Building Courage, Confidence, and Capacity in Learning and Teaching through Student-Faculty Partnership

Building Courage, Confidence, and Capacity in Learning and Teaching through Student-Faculty Partnership

Stories from across Contexts and Arenas of Practice

Edited by
Alison Cook-Sather
Chanelle Wilson

LEXINGTON BOOKS
Lanham • Boulder • New York • London

Published by Lexington Books
An imprint of The Rowman & Littlefield Publishing Group, Inc.
4501 Forbes Boulevard, Suite 200, Lanham, Maryland 20706
www.rowman.com

6 Tinworth Street, London SE11 5AL, United Kingdom

British Library Cataloguing in Publication Information Available

Library of Congress Cataloging-in-Publication Data

Names: Cook-Sather, Alison, 1964– editor.
Title: Building courage, confidence, and capacity in learning and teaching through student-faculty partnership : stories from across contexts and arenas of practice / edited by Alison Cook-Sather, Chanelle Wilson.
Description: Lanham : Lexington Books, [2020] | Includes bibliographical references and index. | Summary: "Co-authored by faculty and students in Canada, England, Hong Kong, Israel, Malaysia, New Zealand, Pakistan, and the United States, the chapters in this book reveal how sustained partnerships focused on pedagogical, curricular, and programmatic development build courage, confidence, and capacity in both student and faculty partners"— Provided by publisher.
Identifiers: LCCN 2020011213 (print) | LCCN 2020011214 (ebook) | ISBN 9781793619587 (cloth) | ISBN 9781793619594 (epub)
Subjects: LCSH: Teacher-student relationships—Cross-cultural studies. | Team learning approach in education—Cross-cultural studies. | Motivation in education—Cross-cultural studies.
Classification: LCC LB1033 .B86 2020 (print) | LCC LB1033 (ebook) | DDC 371.102/3—dc23
LC record available at https://lccn.loc.gov/2020011213
LC ebook record available at https://lccn.loc.gov/2020011214

Contents

Foreword

Kelly E. Matthews

What does it mean to be in pedagogical partnership? How does it feel? What does it sound like? Who decides what happens? Who is learning in pedagogical partnership, how does that learning unfold, and what is being learned? Alison Cook-Sather and Chanelle Wilson have created a space for us to understand the stories of pedagogical partnership—thick descriptions giving life to what it means for students to be constructing pedagogical knowledge together with teaching staff (including faculty/academics, educational developers, librarians). We expect university teaching staff to have pedagogical knowledge and know-how (to what extent that they do is a different story). Yet the pedagogical partnerships described in rich, vivid, and (often) playful detail in this collection clearly reveal students' pedagogical knowledge as well. Taken together, the combined pedagogical knowledge, as demonstrated in the following 10 chapters co-authored by 14 students and 10 teaching staff, extends and exceeds the capacity of individual learners and teachers. I understand why courage is featured as a strong line of sight throughout the book and in the title. It takes courage to challenge the status quo. It takes courage to imagine a different possibility and formation for learning in higher education. It takes courage to enact a different way of being a learner and a teacher that recognizes expertise through experience. It takes courage to name your experience, author your story, and then open yourself up to public gaze and comment.

I read this book with curiosity, and I invite readers to do the same. Curiosity in dialogue means, to me, hearing someone else with respect for their standpoint, appreciating what they are sharing, and then sharing myself by extending, stretching, or viewing the topic of discussion through another lens, rather than comparing, judging, dismissing, or drawing quick conclusions. Read the chapters with curiosity and note the role of curiosity manifested in dialogue through pedagogical partnership stories shared in this work. Take pause, as you read, when your curiosity is piqued to reflect on what is holding your attention and why. There were many moments of clarity for me, as I read, even clarity through contrast. By that, I mean clearer insight into how loose pedagogical partnerships can and should be as a lived practice, yet with a tight and unwavering commitment to intentionally naming learner-teacher relationships in the construction of pedagogical knowledge and praxis.

Alison and Chanelle have opened up another space for dialogue—a place for many voices to come together and enable us (readers) to more thoughtfully understand what it means to be in a pedagogical partnership. By reading with curiosity, we can come into conversations with our 26 storytellers and curators to capture a new clarity regarding pedagogical partnerships.

Acknowledgments

We are grateful to the courageous student and faculty partners who engaged in pedagogical partnership and wrote about it in such honest and thoughtful ways in these chapters. We also wish to thank Holly Buchanan, Megan Conley, and Jessica McCleary for supporting the production of this collection, and Amelia Stieglitz for her assistance with the index.

Introduction

Alison Cook-Sather and Chanelle Wilson

"[Partnership] provided the 'space,' which was the time to focus on . . . how my teaching was matching, or missing, my goals . . . [and] . . . supported the 'bravery' needed to question the traditional boundaries of what is discussed in an undergraduate physics class . . . [and address] . . . social issues in the classroom."—Kerstin Perez, faculty partner (2016)

"This [partnership] program gave me the ability to be brave in multiple settings where I am not only the consultant for my [faculty] partner. . . . I became braver as a person, both in what I am able to do and in sitting peacefully with what is beyond my reach to change."—Anita Ntem, student partner (2016)

When we set out to collect stories of the work of pedagogical partnership from across contexts and arenas of practice, we did not have in mind a theme that would unify the individual contributions to the collection. From our own experiences and from the growing body of scholarship on partnership work, we knew about the strikingly similar outcomes for student and faculty partners, including deepened engagement, raised awareness, and enhanced experiences of teaching and learning (Cook-Sather, Bovill, & Felten, 2014; Matthews, Mercer-Mapstone, Dvorakova, et al., 2019). We also knew that we wanted chapters that would afford readers insight into the lived experiences of partnership work—that would "convey the complexities" of authors' experiences, "including emotions and aspirations," as opposed to presenting a more distanced and abstract set of principles—which is why we call the contributions "stories" (Healey, Matthews, and Cook-Sather, forthcoming). In short, we wanted both content and form that would be compelling and accessible to a diversity of readers interested in pedagogical partnership.

We invited stories from student and faculty pairs or teams in well-established and developing partnership programs, and as the stories started to roll in, we began considering what unifying theme might thread its way through them and offer to readers a generative way of thinking about both the consistent outcomes already documented in the literature, echoed once again in these narratives, and the details of this particular set of stories. We wanted a theme that was in keeping with the premises of partnership—respect, reciprocity, and shared responsibility (Cook-Sather, Bovill, and Felten, 2014)—and we were inspired by chapter authors' use of the word "courage": "it takes courage and vulnerability to work closely with others" (student partner Dionna Jenkins in Wildhagen & Jenkins, this volume); "The partnership . . . provided me the courage to step into a new zone where teaching and learning were a collective enterprise, and I could enrich them with the perspectives of students who have different backgrounds" (faculty author Amrita Kaur in Kaur & Yong Bing, this volume). And we were struck by chapter authors' use of the term "brave": "If you are brave enough to participate in the partnership, then you must be longing for some real and substantive change and that change is not as likely to occur if you stick with what feels comfortable" (faculty partner Amanda Peach, Peach & Ferrell, this volume); and, simply: "first, be brave" (faculty partner Julie Chen and student partner John Ho, Chen & Ho, this volume).

Our own recognition and chapter authors' reiteration of the centrality of courage to partnership prompted us to return to the idea of brave spaces that a student partner had introduced to Alison several years ago and that had been the unifying theme for a collection of essays written by student and faculty partners about their work. The two excerpts with which we open this introduction are drawn from that collection of essays, and the stories in this volume provide rich narratives of what unfolds. Quoted above, Perez (2016), describes "the 'space,' which [is] the time to focus on" teaching and learning through dialogue between student and faculty partners. Such space/time is rare in the lives of both students and faculty, and rarer still is the opportunity to engage in the form of dialogue such space/time affords. As student partner Dionna Jenkins (in Wildhagen & Jenkins, this volume) suggests, we are all socialized from an early age to understand "who our collaborators should be." Pedagogical partnership, she continues, "disrupts this narrative by encouraging people from seemingly different worlds—students and professors—to come together and work toward the common goal of the advancement of teaching and learning."

The dialogue that results from that coming together both supports and fosters the bravery necessary to engage deeply in shared analyses, affirmations, and revisions of teaching and learning that both draw on and develop growth mindset (Cook-Sather, Gauthier, and Foster, 2020). In turn, as Ntem (2016), the other author quoted above, puts it, bravery is supported and fostered "both in what I am able to do and in sitting peacefully with what is beyond my reach to change." We re-evoke this theme of brave spaces and practices to unify the multiple ways in which the stories of student-faculty partnership presented in this collection build courage, confidence, and capacity, and we offer this volume, as a whole, to reaffirm the centrality of drawing on and building courage, confidence, and capacity in learning and teaching through pedagogical partnership. With this volume, we expand the collection of stories of context-specific and partner-particular work, as it unfolds across a diversity of institutions of higher education. And we invite, and hope, this volume inspires further sharing of such stories.

This collection includes ten chapters in which faculty-student pairs or teams tell their own stories of partnership in contexts as various as individual undergraduate courses across the disciplines, a graduate medical school, and institution-wide programs. The institutions in which these stories unfold are small and large, public and private, and research and teaching focused, situated in Aotearoa New Zealand, Canada, England, Hong Kong, Israel, Malaysia, Pakistan, and various regions of the United States. Each story reveals how the brave spaces of student-faculty partnership foster mindsets and practices that support co-creation of learning and teaching experiences that strive to be equitable, engaging, and empowering.

In this introduction, we define pedagogical partnership and introduce ourselves as editors. Then we expand on the concept of brave spaces that serves as the theme unifying the experiences shared in this volume. To prepare readers to dive into the narratives, we preview the stories of learning and teaching in student-faculty partnership included in this collection.

PEDAGOGICAL PARTNERSHIP DEFINED

The definition of student-faculty partnership that underpins this work is "a collaborative, reciprocal process through which all participants have the opportunity to contribute equally, although not necessarily in the same ways, to curricular or pedagogical conceptualization, decision making, implementation, investigation, or analysis" (Cook-Sather, Bovill, & Felten, 2014, pp. 6-7). Key here is the idea of equal, but different, contribution. It's not that each partner contributes the same thing or in the same way; rather, it's that partners' different contributions are valued equally as the partners work together to co-create teaching and learning experiences (Healey et al., 2019). As Matthews et al. (2019) argue, partnership supports dialogue and negotiation and is grounded in the principles of mutual respect and inclusivity—processes that can lead, as Amarachi and Jones (this volume) assert, to equitable partnership.

As an approach, partnership draws on the guiding principles of respect, reciprocity, and shared responsibility (Cook-Sather et al., 2014)—which some scholars of student-faculty partnership recast in "the more explicitly feminist terms of agency, accountability, and affinity" (Cates, Madigan, & Reitenauer, 2018, p. 37)—as well as trust, courage, plurality, authenticity, honesty, inclusivity, and empowerment (Healey, Flint, & Harrington, 2014, pp. 14-15). Enacted within "an ethic of reciprocity"—"a process of balanced give-and-take not of commodities but rather of contributions: perspectives, insights, forms of participation" (Cook-Sather & Felten, 2017, p. 181)— meaningful student-faculty partnership work: (1) fosters inclusive partnerships; (2) nurtures power-sharing relationships through dialogue and reflection; (3) accepts partnership as a process with uncertain outcomes; (4) engages in ethical practices; and (5) enacts partnership for transformation (Matthews, 2017).

All such partnership work endeavors to create spaces and structures to support the development of three groups in higher education. One group is faculty partners as they strive to become the best teachers and learners they can be in their classrooms, departments, and institutions, working to facilitate the learning, sense of belonging, and agency of a diversity of students. Another group is student partners as they take on the role of pedagogical consultant, curriculum co-designer, and co-researcher, deepen their own capacity as learners and agents of change, and contribute to their faculty partners' development and the co-creation of appropriately challenging, equitable, and inclusive classrooms, programs, and institutions. A third group is students enrolled in faculty members' courses, programs, and institutions in maximizing their sense of capacity and agency as learners and people. The spaces and structures of partnership are informed by and must be responsive to complex issues of context, identity, and relationship that can foster or hinder learning, confidence, capacity, sense of belonging, and more.

WHO WE ARE AS EDITORS

We have both experienced numerous pedagogical partnerships, so we know firsthand about the challenges and possibilities of working this way with student partners. We are also at different places in the pedagogical partnership journey, and those different positions afford us different perspectives, both on partnership work itself and on writing about it. This volume came about because Chanelle, in presenting on her partnership work at a conference, was approached by the Acquisitions Editor for Education and Literary Studies at Lexington Books, Holly Buchanan, and invited to submit a proposal for a publication on this work. In the spirit of partnership and in acknowledgement of the context in which she had learned about and experienced the partnership work on which she was reporting, Chanelle asked Alison to work with her on the proposal, which was an extension of Alison's existing scholarship as well as her established practice.

Chanelle is in her first years of the pedagogical partnership journey. She has worked with a student consultant in a qualitative methods course and co-planned and co-taught a course on diversity in higher education in partnership with students, and she has co-authored a reflective essay about her experiences (Wilson & Davis, 2020). As a former K–12 educator, Chanelle has an extensive background in collaborating with colleagues to develop curriculum, and she has also worked closely with students to co-plan school-wide education events. Collaboration comes naturally to her, and she finds the lived experience of partnership essential to informed, equitable, and inclusive pedagogical practice and writing about partnership a critical way to contribute to and create conversations about learning and teaching (Healey et al., 2020).

Alison has directed a pedagogical partnership program for 13 years, supporting over 275 faculty members and 200 student partners in over 380 partnerships. She has also co-planned and co-taught a course on diversity in higher education with a student partner, co-researched pedagogical partnership work with student partners, and co-authored multiple articles, chapters, and five books, three of them with student partners. Before her focus on partnership in college contexts, she facilitated a partnership project that linked secondary and college contexts. This project paired prospective secondary teachers and secondary students in semester-long dialogues to affirm and draw on the secondary students' experiences and insights and to inform the development of the prospective teachers (Cook-Sather, 2002, 2003).

Drawing on our experiences of and through partnership, we endeavored as editors to take a partnership approach both in responding to authors' chapter drafts and in inviting authors to shape the collection beyond contributing their own respective chapters. In our feedback on drafts, we emphasized the importance of balanced voices, being explicit about context and why it matters, and being specific in sharing advice—and why all of these are important in writing about partnership. We also shared all chapter abstracts and our draft introduction with authors and invited them, according to the time and interest they had, to comment on any connections they saw across the Abstracts—themes, patterns, etc.—and anything the Abstracts made them think about for further exploration. Our goal was to support partnership approaches in co-authoring and work in partnership with co-authors to ensure their stories are told and that we provide a coherent experience for readers. The themes chapter authors noted, such as how partners perceived and negotiated hierarchy, informed our discussion of examples of courage, confidence, and capacity in the final chapter of this collection.

PEDAGOGICAL PARTNERSHIPS AS BRAVE SPACES

We opened this introduction with quotes from a faculty and a student partner about partnership as brave space, and we highlight, in this introduction, the bravery of the partners who contributed to this volume—their willingness to engage in this counter-cultural practice, to take risks, to complicate power dynamics, to learn with and from one another. Brian Arao and Kristi Clemens (2013) offer the concept of brave space (as opposed to safe space) as a way to frame dialogue around diversity and social justice. They argue for the use of "brave" rather than "safe" to modify the spaces in which such dialogue unfolds because, as they explain, "to remove risk" from challenging encounters around controversial issues is "simply impossible" (p. 136). To claim we can create "safe space" for such work, Arao and Clemens (2013) argue further, is not only misleading but actually counterproductive: it promises to protect and exempt people from the very difficultness that real learning and growth require and may "encourage entrenchment in privilege" of those, in particular, who think they do not need to make themselves vulnerable (p. 140).

In contrast, brave space implies that there is indeed likely to be danger or harm that require courage to face, but that painful or difficult experiences will be acknowledged and supported, not avoided or eliminated. The concept of brave space "focuses our attention on the active engagement and agency required of participants in spaces intended to support learning"; using "brave" rather than "safe" not only sets a tone for engagement but also proposes a mode of engagement (Cook-Sather, 2016). Within such brave spaces, faculty and student partners alike can build the courage, confidence, and capacity necessary to explore complex and difficult curricular and pedagogical issues and to work toward enacting equitable, engaging, and empowering approaches to teaching and learning. (See Abbott, 2016; Binder, 2016; Ntem, 2016; Perez, 2016; Perez-Putnam, 2016.)

THIS COLLECTION OF STORIES

"The courage to teach," to borrow Parker Palmer's (2009) phrase, is preceded, accompanied, and followed by the courage to analyze, affirm, and revise teaching and learning. In curricular and pedagogical partnership, both faculty and student partners are teachers, and they are also both learners. Over time, relationship-based, teaching-and-learning partnerships can overcome fear, disrupting power dynamics, and stagnancy to support analysis, affirmation, and revision of curricular, pedagogical, and programmatic practice in unique ways. These transformations are articulated in the stories included in this collection, which present a diverse set of extended narratives of the lived experiences of partnership that contextualize insights and reveal how those emerge through partnership. The chapters offer descriptions and analyses of the brave spaces *of* partnership and the brave spaces created *through* partnership. And they offer advice to others for how to maximize the benefits, and navigate the challenges, of curricular, pedagogical, and programmatic partnership for teaching and learning.

While we use the terms "courage," "confidence," and "capacity" to characterize the work, and the outcomes of that work, in the stories included in this volume, these were not terms we offered to authors in our invitation to them to write their chapters. We provided a suggested structure for chapters, but the terms authors used and the particulars of their partnership experiences they chose to share were entirely up to them. The format of chapters is not that of traditional, prescribed academic writing, which can reinforce power dynamics in that it typically requires there to be some authoritative voice. Uncovering and naming power dynamics and writing using a collaborative structure are both elements of partnership work. Co-authors may alternate between individual, first-person perspectives and co-authored sections to share the balanced experience of engaging in partnership. By purposefully structuring the telling of their stories in ways that do not privilege one experience over the other, co-authors mitigate power imbalances and both invoke and enact collaboration.

Each chapter provides context on the specific program and partnership, including who is writing the chapter and how they approached partnership. The focus and goal of the partnership set the stage for how co-authors share their pedagogical partnership experiences. Co-authors share insights *about* working in partnership, and they describe insights gained about teaching about learning *through* working in partnership. These co-authors offer their stories and advice in the hope that others who wish to undertake such partnership may be able to learn from the diverse experiences included in this volume, recognizing at the same time that every partnership is context specific (Healey & Healey, 2018) and participant specific. The act of sharing differing experiences opens up possibilities for new partnership stories to unfold in practice and in presentation.

Through offering ten different versions of the story of partnership, these chapters reveal *how* pedagogical partnership can foster learning, confidence, capacity, and a sense of belonging that contribute to the creation of equitable, engaging, and empowering learning and teaching. We learn how the student-faculty pairs built their relationships—the necessary foundation for trust, understanding, insight, clarification, and, where appropriate, revision. We learn what particular kinds of differences in explorations, analyses, disagreements, dialogues, and more, facilitated insights that led to deepening or revising particular learning and teaching commitments and the development of learning and teaching practices. And we learn from participants themselves what they recommend regarding how others might pursue these benefits and manage the challenges, even as those play out differently in other contexts and relationships.

OVERVIEW OF THE CHAPTERS

Setting the tone for the collection, the volume opens with an example of how differences—of position, perspective, and more—can be resources for student-faculty pedagogical partnership. Chapter 1: The Will to Collaborate across Difference: Mining Difference as a Rich Resource in a Student-Faculty Pedagogical Partnership, by faculty author Tina Wildhagen and student author Dionna Jenkins of Smith College, USA, tells the story of how a faculty-student pair embraced their different perspectives and their disagreements in order to foster a classroom culture where students became collaborators in the collective process of thinking, learning, and feeling.

The three chapters that follow focus on course design and redesign. Chapter 2: Feminist Interventions in Engineering: Co-creating through Conversation, across Disciplines and Identities, by student author Amarachi Chukwu, from the University of Toronto, and faculty author Kim Jones, from McMaster University, both in Canada, narrates how Chukwu and Jones worked together to provide interdisciplinary theoretical grounding, consider power dynamics, and share a range of other insights on teaching a new course entitled "Inclusion in the Engineering Workplace." Chapter 3: A Medical Humanities Curriculum in Medical School: Unexpected Partnerships and Unintended Consequences, by faculty author Julie Chen and student author John Ho of the University of Hong Kong, tells the story of a student and a faculty member whose mutual interest in medical humanities and in developing a positive learning environment led to formal and informal interactions that are influencing the curriculum, teaching and learning culture, and conceptualization of pedagogical partnerships in their medical school. And Chapter 4: Peers and Colleagues: Collaborative Class Design through Student-Faculty Partnerships, by student author Angela Gennocro and faculty author John Straussberger of Florida Gulf Coast University, narrate how their partnership evolved from being primarily focused on observation to embracing curricular co-production.

The next four chapters focus on pedagogical co-creation. Chapter 5: Voicing and Reflecting in a Pedagogical Partnership, by faculty author Doron Narkiss and Iska Naaman of Kaye Academic College, Be'er Sheva, Israel, recounts some of the perceptions of the process both partners underwent and foregrounds the didactic and pedagogical elements of teaching and learning, which are not usually the main concern of either partner. In Chapter 6: The Student-Faculty Partnership Program's Potential for Revitalizing the One-

Shot Library Instruction Session, faculty author Amanda Eugair Peach and student author Ashley Ferrell of Berea College, USA, focus on their work together to revise a pedagogical intervention, the one-shot library instruction session, that is a perennial frustration to faculty, librarians, and students alike. Chapter 7: Untangling the Power Dynamics in Forging Student-Faculty Collaboration, by faculty author Amrita Kaur and student author Toh Yong Bing of Universiti Utara, Malaysia, narrates how this faculty-student pair developed approaches to collaboration that are, in many ways, countercultural in Eastern contexts and generated useful revisions of the psychology course on which they focused. Chapter 8: Student as Co-designer: Processes of Planning and Teaching with the Student in Mind, by faculty author Yasira Waqar and student author Abdul Moeed Asad of Lahore University, Pakistan, describes the ways in which this faculty-student pair revised numerous pedagogical approaches in an education course.

The final two chapters tell stories of student-faculty partnership in programmatic development and redesign. Chapter 9: Learning through Cooperation: Interdisciplinary Insights into Students' Experiences in a Developing Program, by faculty author Katie Quy and student authors Ashly Fuller, Ayushi Kar, Miyama Tada Baldwin, and Omar Hallab at University College London, England, focuses on the ChangeMakers project whose goal was to develop a Social Science student advisory board in two new undergraduate degree programs. Chapter 10: "With Your Basket of Knowledge and My Basket of Knowledge, The People Will Prosper": Learning and Leading in a Student-Staff Partnership Program, by student author Ali Leota and faculty author Kathryn Sutherland at Victoria University of Wellington, Aotearoa New Zealand, describes the thrills and challenges of wider partnership in designing and running the Ako in Action program at Victoria Wellington University, which encourages collective responsibility for learning.

OUR HOPES FOR READERS OF THIS VOLUME

We hope that this collection of stories inspires, encourages, and supports the value of pedagogical partnership. The work described by faculty and student partners from around the globe illustrates the complexities of pedagogical, curricular, and programmatic partnerships and the possibilities of collaboration that disrupts power dynamics, convenes diverse perspectives, and works toward a common goal. There is an intersectional relationship between the courage, confidence, and capacity that chapter contributors share in their stories: one may develop from the other, serve as the reinforcement for the other, or be the thread that runs through them all. The nuances in experiences highlight the fact that no two partnerships need look the same, and no group of people within one classroom or institution will bring the same perspective.

But, when brave space is created for partnership geared toward growth, and when divergent voices are invited to contribute, respected, and affirmed, the potential for generative inquiry is endless, especially when centering teaching and learning as the beneficiary of student-faculty partnerships.

REFERENCES

Abbott, C. (2016). Leaping and landing in brave spaces. *Teaching and Learning Together in Higher Education, 18.* https://repository.brynmawr.edu/tlthe/vol1/iss18/4

Arao, B., & Clemens, K. (2013). From safe spaces to brave spaces: A new way to frame dialogue around diversity and social justice. In L. M. Landreman (Ed.), *The art of effective facilitation* (pp. 135-150). Stylus Publishing, LLC.

Binder, C. (2016). Practicing virtue in teaching and learning. *Teaching and Learning Together in Higher Education, 18.* https://repository.brynmawr.edu/tlthe/vol1/iss18/5

Cates, R. M., Madigan, M. R., & Reitenauer, V. L. (2018). "Locations of possibility": Critical perspectives on partnership. *International Journal for Students as Partners, 2*(1), 33-46. https://doi.org/10.15173/ijsap.v2i1.3341.

Cook-Sather, A. (2016). Creating brave spaces within and through student-faculty pedagogical partnerships. *Teaching and Learning Together in Higher Education, 18.* http://repository.brynmawr.edu/tlthe/vol1/iss18/1

Cook-Sather, A. (2003). Movements of mind: *The Matrix*, metaphors, and re-imagining Education. *Teachers College Record, 105*(6), 946-977.

Cook-Sather, A. (2002). Re(in)forming the conversations: Student position, power, and voice in teacher education. *Radical Teacher, 64,* 21-28.

Cook-Sather, A., Bovill, C., & Felten, P. (2014). *Engaging students as partners in learning and teaching: A guide for faculty.* San Francisco: Jossey-Bass.

Cook-Sather, A., & Felten, P. (2017). Ethics of academic leadership: Guiding learning and teaching. In F. Su & M. Wood (Eds.), *Cosmopolitan perspectives on academic leadership in higher education* (pp. 175–191). London: Bloomsbury Academic.

Cook-Sather, A., Gauthier, L., & Foster. (2020). The role of growth mindset in developing pedagogical partnership programs: Findings from a cross-institutional study. *Journal of Innovation, Partnership and Change 6*(1). https://journals.studentengagement.org.uk/index.php/studentchangeagents/article/view/1004

Healey, M., Matthews, K. E., & Cook-Sather, A. (2020). *Writing about learning and teaching in higher education: Contributing to scholarly conversations across a range of genres.* Elon University Center for Engaged Learning Open Access Series.

Healey, M., & Healey, R. (2018). "It depends": Exploring the context-dependent nature of students as partners' practices and policies. *International Journal for Students as Partners, 2*(1), 1–10. https://doi.org/10.15173/ijsap.v2i1.3472

Healey, R. L., Lerczak, A., Welsh, K., & France, D. (2019). By any other name? The impacts of differing assumptions, expectations, and misconceptions in bringing about resistance to staff-student partnership. *International Journal for Students as Partners, 3*(1).

Healey, M., Flint, A., & Harrington, K. (2014). *Students as partners in learning and teaching in higher education.* York: Higher Education Academy.

Matthews, K. E. (2017). Five propositions for genuine students as partners practice. *International Journal of Students as Partners, 1*(2).

Matthews, K. E., Mercer-Mapstone, L., Dvorakova, S., Acai, A., Cook-Sather, A., Felten, P., Healey, M., Healey, R., & Marquis, E. (2019). Enhancing outcomes and reducing inhibitors to the engagement of students and staff in learning and teaching partnerships: Implications for academic development. *International Journal for Academic Development, 24*(3), 246-259. DOI: 10.1080/1360144X.2018.1545233

Ntem, A. (2016). Learning to be brave within and beyond partnership. *Teaching and Learning Together in Higher Education,18.* http://repository.brynmawr.edu/tlthe/vol1/iss18/6

Palmer, P. (2009). *The courage to teach.* Hoboken, NJ: John Wiley & Sons.

Perez, K. (2016). Striving toward a space for equity and inclusion in physics classrooms. *Teaching and Learning Together in Higher Education, 18.* https://repository.brynmawr.edu/tlthe/vol1/iss18/3

Perez-Putnam, M. M. (2016). Belonging and brave space as hope for personal and institutional inclusion. *Teaching and Learning Together in Higher Education, 18.* https://repository.brynmawr.edu/tlthe/vol1/iss18/2

Wilson, C., & Davis, M. (2020). Transforming the student-professor relationship: A multiphase research partnership. *International Journal for Students as Partners* 4(1), 155–161. https://doi.org/10.15173/ijsap.v4i1.3913

Chapter One

The Will to Collaborate across Difference

Mining Difference as a Rich Resource in a Student-Faculty Pedagogical Partnership

Tina Wildhagen and Dionna Jenkins

CONTEXT

Provided by Floyd Cheung, Director of the Sherrerd Center for Teaching and Learning.

Established in 2016 and initially funded by a grant from the Andrew W. Mellon Foundation, the Student-Faculty Pedagogical Partnership Program at Smith College pairs faculty members who wish to reflect on their teaching with student partners who can offer their perspective as non-participant observers once a week for an entire semester. The faculty members learn about partnership through a workshop based on the principles and experiences described in the book *Engaging Students as Partners in Learning and Teaching* by Alison Cook-Sather, Catherine Bovill, and Peter Felten. They are supported during the semester by consultations with the Director of the Sherrerd Center for Teaching and Learning and a Sherrerd Teaching Mentor. In addition, they support one another by meeting as a group occasionally. The students take a once-a-week, two-credit class, IDP210: The Pedagogy of Student-Faculty Partnership, to learn theories of teaching and learning and to discuss their partnerships under conditions of strict confidentiality. Either the Director or the Mentor teaches this class, depending on availability. The Sherrerd Center supports five to eight partnerships per semester.

SETTING THE SCENE: A GLIMPSE INTO OUR
PARTNERSHIP WORK (DIONNA)

It's a typical Monday. Tina and I sit in her second floor office reflecting on last week's classes and briefly go over a rough plan for what we'll have students do that day. We're about halfway through our usual hour together. As I put my notes away, she turns back to me and says, "Oh, yeah, what did you scope out from last week?"

I can't believe I'd almost forgotten about it. During our last handful of meetings, Tina and I had agreed that I should sit in a back corner of the classroom for a day so I could keep an eye on student laptop activity, as we both suspected that some students had recently been using their electronic devices to disengage from class. I search my memory for what I had observed the week before. "Saw some Facebook, some emails being written. Typical stuff."

It's difficult news to hear, just as much as it is difficult to report. Tina shares her frustrations, telling me that it is disheartening to be open to students' preferences and accommodations only to have some of them take advantage of it. Of course, I understand—it sometimes annoys me as a student in my own classes—but it's also something I've learned to tune out. I think: It happens all the time, and as long as it's not a major distraction, why be bothered by it? "Oh, Tina, stop being old," I quip. "It's a sign of the times. You just have to deal with it."

And so begins the conversation. We go back and forth about electronic devices and some students' tendency to use social media during class. I say it's inevitable and that each individual is charged with keeping tabs on their own learning, regardless of what others do; she sees my point but maintains that it still hampers the collective learning process that is central to her teaching philosophy and overall classroom culture. I maintain my stance, but the longer I listen, the more I see the validity of her perspective. It becomes obvious that we see this issue differently. Instead of trying to reconcile our differences, we decide to lean into them and invite our students into the conversation. We will hold a discussion in class about how our students understand "off-task" technology use in the classroom. What does it mean to them? Why do they do it? How do they think the teacher understands it? We resolve to keep from getting mired in the apparent oppositional positions of students and teachers on this issue: teachers as (mostly) non-digital natives committed to extinguishing a rude and disruptive behavior and students as (mostly) digital natives who might engage in this behavior for reasons completely unforeseen by teachers.

The discussion with our students yields many useful insights that we incorporate into the fabric of the class. For example, we learned from our students that they are sometimes competing for work shifts that must be claimed online. If they miss the opportunity to claim the shift during class, they have missed an opportunity to earn much-needed extra money. A short electronics break in the middle of the class acknowledges the ever-increasing pressure on young people to be connected at all times.

INTRODUCTION (DIONNA AND TINA)

As the opening vignette illustrates, the discussion about students' use of electronic devices in class, and the resulting plan for our next class, exemplifies the greatest lesson of our partnership—that differences between students and teachers need not function as impediments to fruitful teaching and learning experiences. Instead, differences can reveal opportunities for teachers and students to learn from each other. In this chapter, we reflect on some ways in which our differences manifested in the partnership and how we tried to use them to improve the teaching and learning experience for everyone.

The main goal of our partnership was to encourage active participation of all members in a discussion-oriented class. Our approach was to observe and listen closely to learn from the students in the room about what worked, what didn't, and why. Every week we met to reflect on the class we'd just had and plan how to implement the lessons we'd learned in future classes. Each example we share in this chapter illustrates how we embraced differences in the service of improving teaching and learning.

WHAT WE LEARNED ABOUT WORKING IN PARTNERSHIP: WHO IS AN APPROPRIATE PARTNER?

Dionna: Collaboration is an odd subject for me, considering that I have historically been the kind of person who prefers to work independently. I think this is because most of the partnerships I have been a part of in the past have been involuntary, either as part of a school assignment or within a similar context that is often conducive to transactional interaction. Being a pedagogical partner forced me to re-examine my perceptions of collaboration, particularly in terms of what it means to work with another person.

It seems that we have generally confined the idea of working "in partnership" with someone to a distinctly compartmentalized space—to collaborate means to work with someone similar in status, position, background, and understanding of the work they are charged with doing. This perception is not surprising, given the normalization of such thinking through practices within schools and various sectors of the workforce. Simply put, it is made clear to us, even at the earliest stages of life, who our collaborators should be. The pedagogical partnership disrupts this narrative by encouraging people from seemingly different worlds—students and professors—to come together and work toward the common goal of the advancement of teaching and learning.

One would think that Tina and I, with our different positions on campus as professor and student, would often disagree on observations made during the course of our work together. There is some truth to this—different people are bound to see things differently at one point or another—but it is those differences, along with a commitment to learn from each other, that contributed to our success as pedagogical partners. Having the will to collaborate across difference and be open to new perspectives allowed us to see our partnership, as well as our work as individuals, in a mostly unforeseen light. When we put our thoughts and knowledge together, we were able to tap into a new method of problem solving that neither of us could have discovered alone. With combined power, we enhanced our individual strengths and our dedication to the work put before us, creating an impactful learning experience for students and one that gave us a deeper appreciation for the rewards and challenges of team work.

Tina: I think of myself as someone who likes to work alone, too. Most teachers accomplish the work of teaching primarily alone. We plan our course, show up to class alone and teach our students, and grade students' work alone. This was my view of teaching when I was a student, and this is how I taught for much of my teaching career.

Before working in pedagogical partnerships with students, the thought of partnering with a student in my teaching was simply unthinkable. It never occurred to me that this would have been possible or desirable. Before learning about the partnership program at Smith, I had never heard of partnering with a student to work on pedagogy. Like most of my colleagues, my considerations of students as involved in teaching focused on traditional teaching assistants who help with grading or run study groups. Just as Dionna notes, engaging in pedagogical partnerships with students has challenged my notions of who might make an appropriate partner. Students bring insights to the partnership that I simply could not have on my own. Through my work with Dionna, I have learned that collaboration across traditional structural and cultural boundaries, the very thing that invites skepticism in some, is itself a rich resource to be mined.

WHAT OUR PARTNERSHIP TAUGHT US: THE VALUE OF ACTIVE REFLECTION, IMPROVISATION, AND PREPARATION

Tina: Working in a pedagogical partnership has taught me that teaching alone does not necessarily invite active reflection during the semester. There are ways to reflect on one's teaching in real time when one is teaching a course alone, but teaching alone does not *require* this reflection. When I teach alone, I make earnest efforts to reflect on how certain strategies are working or how students are doing with the material, but these frequently end up feeling like a side project that can siphon energy away from the main event of teaching.

By contrast, teaching in partnership positions active and collaborative reflection front-and-center in the teaching process. Teaching in partnership changes the game. Active reflection is no longer an option that the teacher may take up as she wishes; it becomes a mandate. This is made possible because on a regular basis, the partners meet to reflect, considering: How are things going in the class? How are the students engaging with the material? What works? What does not work? Can we understand why?

Dionna: Working with Tina allowed me to imagine greater possibilities of what partnership can look like, as well as my own capabilities as a partner. We came into this with the intention to work inductively, identifying the focus of our collaboration over time and fine-tuning it further as we went along. This was new to me (I'm a planner), but I gradually began to see just how valuable of a tactic it is. By not having a pre-determined plan, we were forced to observe and notice pretty much *everything*, a task that is equal parts daunting and rewarding. We started not knowing exactly what we were looking for, but once we began to notice patterns, ideas began to form and concrete strategies were quick to emerge. I found myself thinking in ways that I hadn't before. It wasn't a traditional methodology, but it worked just the same. This is one of the greatest benefits of working in a partnership—we got to take risks by adopting new approaches to problem solving and witness our own adapting in the process.

Tina: Dionna is right. I tend to take an improvisational approach to my teaching, drawing on my toolkit of teaching skills, stocked heavily with the craft knowledge that I have accumulated over more than a decade teaching college students. The partnership with Dionna surfaced what I had long had a sense of, but could never quite put my finger on—that combining craft knowledge and formal knowledge from the learning sciences can lead to something really special in the classroom.

As a requirement of this partnership, Dionna was enrolled in a course in which she learned about teaching from the learning sciences. She brought insights from this formal study to the reflective process in our partnership. I brought the craft knowledge that I have built over many years of college teaching. We would put it together, and very interesting new insights often emerged.

For example, in class one day I spontaneously presented students with what I called a puzzle. We hadn't studied anything about this puzzle formally, but I invited students to discuss why they thought the puzzle existed and posit possible solutions. During our meeting following that class, Dionna shared with me that what I had done was a bit like something she'd read about in her class, the strategy of presenting an area of content to students before the students have formally studied anything about that content. The idea is to let students organically foster their own understanding without preliminary direction from reading material or instructor input. She shared with me some of what research suggests about why this works for learners. Now I have a new tool in my teaching toolkit. This is no longer something that I might try on the fly, mostly following instinct, but a more formal teaching tool that I can intentionally build into the plan for a class.

OUR PARTNERSHIP: A MESSY, REWARDING COLLABORATIVE PROJECT

Dionna: Teaching and learning is messy, something that I have known for quite a while but never deeply understood, until engaging in this partnership. I use the word "messy" to mean a variety of things—not just the unpredictability of teaching, but also the careful reflection, consideration, and planning that goes on behind the scenes. At the heart of messiness, I think, lies patience. This includes patience with oneself, one's partner, and the process of the partnership itself. It takes courage and vulnerability to work closely with others, as well as a willingness to have one's strengths, weaknesses, and uncertainties amplified on a regular basis. All of this forced me to put much thought into what I believe were major overarching questions throughout this process: What can I bring to the table to best serve this partnership? What does it mean for me to be successful in that? The answer to both questions mostly came in the form of me continuing to venture on, even when I thought I was incapable of doing so and had no idea where it would lead. I am not an expert on pedagogy, nor had I ever taken a class in the learning sciences before I began the partnership. Because of this, whenever challenges arose in my role as a student partner, I often felt unqualified and unable to even begin looking for solutions. And sometimes, even when I simply *thought* I had something new to introduce, I would question whether it was "good enough" to share with Tina.

I remember thinking: I'm just a kid—do I even know what I'm doing? And at the same time: shouldn't this be easier? Looking back, this dissonance is an especially frustrating catch-22. Students at Smith agree to do this partnership because they want to help their professors and because their professors have faith in their abilities. Students *want* to do this work well and believe, in some way or another, that they can do so. But I think it is the yearning to do well that fuels uncertainty. Self-doubt is not uncommon at a place like Smith, but only when one has the patience with oneself to recognize this feeling and work through it can the most rewarding aspects of partnership be realized. It was counterproductive for me to dwell in thoughts of inadequacy. Tina and I think differently not only because of our different positions as professor and student, but also because we are different people. Embracing our differences helped me overcome my discomfort and begin to trust myself to be the "expert" in the room just as much as I trusted Tina. It was messy, but definitely worth it.

This is why I think engaging in student-faculty partnership is so invaluable. The average undergrad is typically not granted many opportunities to do work that challenges them in ways they had not encountered before, as well as gain inside access to the seemingly mystifying intellectual world of a college professor. To be honest, I was surprised that the pedagogical partnership even existed at Smith and was inspired by initiatives at other colleges. I had been under the impression for some time that teaching in higher education was not as big an area of concern as it is in K-12 settings. When I was much younger, I thought that classroom experiences in college were mostly impersonal and that it was a professor's responsibility to drill knowledge into a student's brain in the most cut-and-dried way possible. I grew out of these assumptions upon navigating my first year of college, but even then and until I became a pedagogical partner, I was mostly unaware of how much time, thought, and energy goes into postsecondary teaching just as it does at any level.

Tina: What I have learned through working in partnership with Dionna is that active reflection introduces the possibility for teaching to become the thing that it should be: an ongoing project between teachers and students, open to improvisation, revision, and reflection. A beautiful thing happens in an effective partnership. Not only are the professor and student partners actively reflecting on teaching, but the students in the class begin to do so, as well. The students come to see themselves as partners in the project of the class rather than passive recipients of the material prepared by the professor.

For me, the "messiness" to which Dionna refers means that this process of active reflection will not always proceed with ease. Because of our different vantage points—Dionna as student and me as professor—different sets of assumptions often undergirded our own reflections. For example, I assumed that using electronic devices in class for non-class related tasks meant that students had disengaged, while Dionna assumed that it meant they were multi-tasking. Only once we identified the assumptions underlying each of our reflections and discussed how and why they differed could our reflections become generative.

TALKING ABOUT TALKING

Tina: A critical lesson from this partnership was that explicitly inviting students into the process of teaching and learning can be transformative for students and teachers alike. As a student myself, I never gave much thought to how professors went about making plans for class, or why they made the decisions that they did. That was their job, and mine was to show up and perform. Teaching in partnership draws back the curtain that obscures the teaching process because, by definition, it shows students that the teacher is actively working on the teaching process. Our most tangible achievement in this regard was "Talking about Talking," an idea that we stumbled upon during one of our weekly meetings. Dionna and I were discussing the apparent limits of increasing student participation by encouraging them to do so during class or one-on-one conversations. Then we hit on it: Let's move that discussion outside of the class!

Dionna: We decided to invite a small group of self-selecting students to an informal out-of-class discussion (aptly named "Talking About Talking") in which we all talked together about the experience of speaking in a classroom. A mixture of both relatively talkative and quiet students came to the discussion, and we had a fruitful conversation about specific factors that either help or hinder participation. We also discussed what we all thought a truly meaningful classroom experience should be.

Tina: The "Talking about Talking" event proved to be a fruitful discussion about how all of us could work together to foster student participation. At our next class meeting, the participants debriefed the rest of the class on our discussion, inviting all members of the class to partake in a dialogue about what works, what doesn't, and why when it comes to participating in class.

Dionna: My role as a student partner, but not being a student in the class, put me in an interesting position for "Talking about Talking." I was able to hear and perceive course students' thoughts through an analytical lens, while at the same time being able to empathize and connect their experiences to my own. I was able to see this group discussion as both useful data and a prime example of what can happen when teachers make the effort to engage students' perspectives, so they can figure out better ways to help them succeed.

This was the first time in my college career that I had seen a professor take such a grand step to gauge student insight. After the "Talking about Talking" discussion, I noticed a gradual change in the quiet students who had taken part, as well as in some who hadn't. Some days were better than others, but in general, these students showed greater active participation and began to steer class discussions in new directions. I doubt that this would have happened if we hadn't done "Talking About Talking." It was through that experience that I saw how much of an impact instructors can have on students' learning experiences, if they take the time to meet them where they are.

ADVICE FOR NEW PARTNERS

Tina: My biggest advice for those entering into a partnership is to practice being open and flexible. And this cannot just be a state of mind; it has to be a practice, something that is consistently and consciously *done*. Both parties must feel free to share their ideas with the other in the spirit of collaboration. If doing the partnership the right way, there will be disagreements sometimes, and those disagreements will produce useful lessons. Dionna and I found that these differences became productive when they allowed us to identify the tacit assumptions that we brought to our work. We could then consciously decide whether those assumptions were misguided, useful, or in need of modification.

Dionna: Trust the process and don't underestimate yourself! Great things can happen when people learn to take everything in as it comes and do their best to make the most of it. I came into this partnership more fearful than I would like to admit. What could I, a typical bright-eyed undergrad, possibly have to offer a professor who had already proven herself to be one of the most influential instructors on campus? I subconsciously held onto this fear for some time, but as the semester progressed I grew more comfortable allowing myself to just take a chance and let my ideas flow. In the end, I began to see that differences between partners are nothing to fear. The level of authority or expertise that either party brings to the table should not dictate the terms of the partnership. The most important aspect of partnership is for both parties to consistently learn from each other and use their strengths to yield good ideas. Of course, all partners will not always come up with something absolutely brilliant, nor should that be the expectation. The main goal should be to do good work and to learn something along the way, a goal that is definitely achievable if the spirit of the partnership is kept at heart.

Chapter Two

Feminist Interventions in Engineering

Co-creating through Conversation, across Disciplines and Identities

Amarachi Chukwu and Kim Jones

CONTEXT

Provided by Beth Marquis, Associate Director (Research) at the Paul R. MacPherson Institute for Leadership, Innovation, and Excellence in Teaching

McMaster University's Student Partners Program was co-developed by the university's central teaching and learning institute and the interdisciplinary Arts & Science program in 2013. It aims to develop and support opportunities for students and faculty/staff at the university to collaborate meaningfully on a wide range of teaching and learning projects, including course (re)design, curriculum review, and teaching and learning scholarship. Faculty, students, and staff across the university are invited to submit projects three times a year, and successful submissions receive funding that pays students for the time they spend working on the project, as well as additional support from the teaching and learning institute. Currently, more than 200 students (undergraduate and graduate), faculty, and staff participate in the program each year.

Who are We and What Motivated Our Partnership?

Kim Jones, an Associate Professor in Chemical Engineering at McMaster University, had proposed a new course on Inclusion in the Engineering Workplace, and she felt she could benefit from the content expertise and perspective of a student partner who had a background in diversity and inclusion work to develop it. Amarachi Chukwu, a Master's student in Gender Studies and Feminist Research, came across the Student Partners Program among the onslaught of emails graduate students routinely receive and was intrigued by the collaborative nature of the project. She became very interested in the idea of learning about course creation through hands-on experience, but the engineering course seemed out of her area of knowledge; however, after meeting to discuss the goals of the course, she decided to join the project.

As part of the application process to participate in McMaster University's Student Partners Program, Amarachi was expected to choose and rank the top three projects she was interested in working on. She initially ranked this partnership as her second, not her first, choice because the field of Engineering was relatively unknown to her despite interest in the project, but Kim believed that her background and expertise would make her a potentially perfect match. Kim viewed the interview as a chance to see if Amarachi would share her vision for making inclusion a reality in Engineering, and a half-hour interview turned into a three-hour conversation. Although this was not our intention, upon reflection, we both believe that our ongoing conversations were an essential component in our effective partnership. Therefore, the rest of the chapter is structured as a conversation.

Kim: In addition to my role in Chemical Engineering, I am the Chair of the Ontario Network of Women in Engineering, an organization that facilitates cooperative efforts and programming at universities across Canada to improve the representation of women in undergraduate engineering programs. I am also the Chair of McMaster University's Women in Engineering Committee and served as an Engineering Leadership Fellow to advance equity, diversity, and inclusion.

I am a lifelong feminist. My mother has an undergraduate degree in pure mathematics, a master's degree in computer science (obtained in the 1960s), and an MBA. My father is an electrical engineer with a master's degree who also identifies as a feminist, and I have many strong female role models in my family.

My background is one of privilege. I am a white, cis-gender, heterosexual, non-disabled woman who believes strongly in social justice. I have also experienced sexism in forms that vary from overt and personal to subtly biased and systemic. I had co-op work terms in the 1990s in which I observed both blatant and unintentional sexism that led me to temporarily abandon engineering and complete my master's degree in another field. When I started as an engineering professor at McMaster in 2003, I was one of only five female faculty members out of approximately 140 in engineering. There, the discrimination I experienced was rarely intentional, but resulted from low representation, implicit bias, and systemic structural inequalities.

As I became more involved with advocacy for underrepresented groups in engineering, I began to identify barriers to recruiting and retaining women in the engineering profession. Women are more likely than men to leave the engineering profession, and one key reason is "chilly work environment." This directly affects women practicing in the field, but also capable, qualified, high school girls (and their parents) who perceive that their considerable talents and intelligence might be best applied outside engineering. I was motivated to find ways that the university could influence these work environments and give tools of success to students who were likely to experience inequities and unwelcoming work environments.

I thought that offering a course in pursuit of these goals would make space for students to engage for credit, whereas workshops are typically an "extra" that can be difficult to prioritize. In engineering in Canada, students are required to take several non-technical courses called complementary studies electives. My proposed course would be offered within engineering but count as one of these electives. I did not want it to be a mandatory part of the program because mandatory equity, diversity, and inclusion training often has backlash effects and because it is challenging to scale up controversial discussions to large groups.

When I first proposed this idea for a new course, I was focused on providing tools to help women overcome barriers they were likely to face in the workplace. I initially received significant pushback from the faculty's administration: they were concerned that men would be excluded, that positing gender as a binary was not inclusive, and that women were not the only people to suffer discrimination in the workplace. Indeed, recent research has shown that highlighting tools for women to use to overcome structural inequities leads to a belief that the inequities are the fault of the women and that women must change themselves rather than a belief that we as a society should all work to address the unfair structures. Similarly, many individuals are keen to act as allies, but do not have the tools or knowledge to do so. It is also very true that many groups experience inequities in engineering workplaces.

I decided to respond to this feedback by restructuring the course to include some theoretical context, considerations of structural barriers and possible systematic changes combined with individual actions that would be effective for those who experience discrimination and by their allies. I recognized that I needed help to do this well. The perspective of a student would ensure that the course achieved its objectives in a meaningful way. If the student could bring expertise in both the subject matter and the mode of delivery, I thought, that would be ideal. I have only taught engineering courses, which tend to be delivered quite differently from discussion-based humanities courses. Thus, I was eager to partner with a student who could bring interdisciplinary experience, and even better if the student could bring the perspective of a social location different from my own.

Amarachi: At the time of this partnership, I was finishing my Master's in Gender Studies and Feminist Research. I was looking for an opportunity to work in the university while doing an Independent Research project with no clear idea of what exactly I was looking for, when I found out about the student-faculty partnerships. As a graduate student hoping to become a teacher, I thought the student-faculty partnership could be a unique chance to engage directly with a professor in course creation and learn more about pedagogical practices that were intentional and critical of existing processes and limitations. As a black woman in academia, I have had many conversations about thriving in spaces like the academy that are not necessarily invested in my success and have been deeply interested in how—through course creation, citational practice, and curriculum design—all educators can engage in radical pedagogy that centers students from minoritized groups whose specific experiences and lives are rarely acknowledged.

Although this partnership was not my first choice because engineering felt wholly outside my sphere of knowledge, it was also deeply intriguing to me as a feminist working in the field of gender studies because of the important re-centering of women in a field long known to assume maleness as its subject and erase women. As a Nigerian woman in the diaspora, my background also played a role in my interest in the project. One of the many existing stereotypes held within the community was that almost all Nigerian men and boys seemed to end up in engineering no matter where they were in the world. Although I know this desire for children, especially immigrant children, to be in fields like engineering was not necessarily unique to Nigerian parents, the prevalence of people within that field in my community meant that I knew a lot of people whose lives were unfolding in that sphere and whose experiences by virtue of being from minoritized racial and/or gender groups were influenced by the engineering environment daily.

My father was an engineer before his recent retirement, and my brother was in university obtaining his mechanical engineering bachelor's degree, and despite my not sharing an interest in the specificity of their work, we often discussed their experiences and the social context of their field. My experience in conversations with friends and family in engineering tended either to deem social issues as irrelevant because sciences were beyond that or to consider the seemingly toxic social dynamics as inextricable from the environment and an obstacle that one merely had to overcome.

Kim's project focusing on a course that sought to go past performative discussion on diversity to critique, strategize, and intervene in the engineering field was therefore a necessary and worthwhile project in service of creating an inclusive environment that I wanted to see more of. Although I wasn't initially sure what I could contribute to the partnership, being from a humanities field, all of these factors made me choose it as one of my top three potential student partner projects.

How Did the Partnership Unfold and What Insights Did We Gain about Partnership?

Early conversation built trust; dialogue became knowledge production.

Kim: I didn't intentionally structure our first interview as a conversation, but I did want to ensure I effectively communicated my passion for the project. Particularly given the equity-linked goals, I thought it was important that any student partner shared my purpose. Even if our "interview" had been our only interaction, it was valuable, because you were so open to sharing ideas.

Amarachi: I didn't exactly know what to expect coming into the initial meeting, but my interest and passion for equity work in all its iterations meant I had to explore this opportunity, and that passion was immediately reflected from you in our conversation.

Kim: Our initial conversation really built the basis for our subsequent interactions. Even though we were accomplishing our goals, I also felt like I was just having a fun and intellectually challenging chat with a friend. The trust we established in that first conversation made it easy to bring up even difficult topics, and I looked forward to our weekly meetings. Our discussions were so different from those I normally have with my colleagues, and I valued the space to share my thoughts with someone who "got it" and could phrase things in a more articulate, informed way than I could.

Amarachi: I didn't always feel articulate, but I felt the same excitement about our conversations and felt comfortable thinking out loud and stumbling through some thoughts at times. The conversations we were having were fun, eye-opening, and interesting in themselves and were made even better by imagining students getting an opportunity to similarly engage with the topics we passionately discussed every week—we knew these would have an impact on their lives. Although conversations about equity were part of being in my field, the specific context of engineering was foreign in many ways. Despite our discussion on how I had family and friends in the field and thought this course was necessary, I remember telling you I didn't choose this project as my first choice because I was unsure of my value in the partnership since I did not know the specific experiences of marginalized groups within the engineering field. Your response that you had the lived experience and could offer that to the partnership, and I had other knowledges to offer that were valuable, really made a difference. It allowed me to see that our imagined gaps in knowledge and points of 'expertise' were complementary, and working together would allow for those different perspectives to be in dialogue in service of the course.

Kim: I came to this work essentially as a curious, motivated amateur. I have not had the privilege of formal education in this area, so I am not perfectly confident in my own grasp of current feminist theory. I made this very clear in our first meeting, which I believe made space for you to share your own expertise and become a much more equal partner. I have also found that when working in equity, diversity, and inclusion there is always more to learn, and that humility and willingness to ask questions and recognize your own limitations is critically important.

Amarachi: I believe the act of sharing our mutual concern of not knowing enough about aspects that were necessary to make the course was a moment of vulnerability from the beginning that established trust. The open conversation we started with complicated the generally implicit teacher-student power dynamic as we both conceived ourselves as knowers and learners simultaneously in this scenario. This meant that we came into the conversation aware that we had blind spots and open to having them pointed out even when they were uncomfortable.

INTERDISCIPLINARITY HELPED OVERCOME POWER IMBALANCES

Kim: Our different disciplinary backgrounds helped us both learn from each other, which added to the richness of our conversations.

Amarachi: I think the fact of our different academic backgrounds made it possible to circumvent the faculty-student power dynamic to some extent. Coming into the first meeting, I was less nervous because I had no existing prior relationship and felt that if anything became uncomfortable or it didn't work out, there would be no consequences, so that facilitated open and easy conversation. I became comfortable going into the partnership, confident that I could contribute from my knowledge as a student in the humanities who had taken many courses and had defined opinions on what motivated student engagement beyond surface content learning for the primary purpose of getting good grades. The disruption of the implicit power imbalance by virtue of our different fields allowed me to be completely transparent about my experiences as a student engaging in discussions around the topics we were proposing.

Kim: Discussion of power is so important in partnership programs. I had previously participated in our student partner program (focusing on course refinement, not development). My student partner worked hard, but she was still an undergraduate student in our Chemical Engineering program, working on a course that I had previously taught her. Despite my best efforts, our relationship was much less balanced. She mostly looked to me for guidance and was reluctant to offer her own ideas. As a result, her contributions were superficial compared to yours. I think once a power relationship has been established (for example by teaching a student), it takes a very special person to step outside of those established constraints. That you were working in a different discipline meant that there was no existing power relationship, which was very helpful. I suspect it also helped that you were in graduate school and beginning to recognize your own value as an independent scholar.

STRUCTURE FACILITATED PRODUCTIVITY – THE RELATIONSHIP WAS EQUITABLE BUT NOT EQUAL

Kim: Speaking of power, we can't pretend we had the same role. I defined the initial problem and ensured there were clearly articulated expectations (action items) at the end of each of our weekly meetings. I am also the one who will ultimately have to teach the course and who had to advocate for its inclusion in the curriculum. This setting of specific tasks, including suggesting feminist theory to contextualize the topics in the original outline, finding appropriate resources and readings, and proposing assessments, was helpful for us both because we had many other constraints on our time. Student partners, by definition, have other pressing demands on their time and should prioritize their schoolwork. We needed to carve out time for the partnership work, but I also had to be respectful of a student's primary mission: getting a degree.

Amarachi: The tasks at the end of each meeting were necessary in ensuring the project was progressing and the partnership was productive. However, it did not feel like tasks assigned to an assistant or subordinate, but rather tasks that were agreed upon mutually in conversation. Points of interests or inquiry that I brought up in conversation were part of the tasks that were set on the agenda. The reality of our different positions and experiences also meant that I was not fully comfortable working without a clear structure and needed guidance in this new experience of creating a course. This, however, did not make me feel subordinate and is where I would make the distinction between an equal versus equitable partnership, with the latter being more in line with our experience. I make that distinction because I felt that in our partnership there was always effort expended to reiterate the value of my ideas and make space for me in conversations that I might not necessarily have taken otherwise, if I perceived my role as one of assistance not collaboration. The extra support and resources you provided for me in recognition that I had never done anything in course design, allowed me to engage more meaningfully in the course creation process, exemplifying an equitable partnership.

Kim: Absolutely! It was important to me that you knew that I valued your contributions, while recognizing that our roles and teaching experience were somewhat different. We brought different backgrounds and skill sets to the table. I learned a lot of theoretical content and perspectives from you (and from your shared experience) that were invaluable. I also needed to learn from you about different ways of transferring knowledge to students (that came from your humanities background).

STUDENT PARTNERS EVOLVE FROM CONSUMERS TO PRODUCERS OF KNOWLEDGE

Kim: I also think you evolved through the process.

Amarachi: I definitely did! The partnership was a transformational point for me in transitioning from seeing myself as a student whose role is to absorb knowledge from teachers/professors who hold all the knowledge, to envisioning myself as knowledge holder and producer. The growth experience that was occurring throughout my graduate school experience began this shift, but the partnership reaffirmed that for me, because I had the opportunity and ability to contribute individually and speak to gaps in knowledge while still learning. This process helped build my confidence in myself as a valuable contributor, even when I don't hold all the knowledge.

Kim: I think we sometimes don't recognize that students don't automatically have the confidence to picture themselves as developers of knowledge. The professor's role in this partnership is to help develop that ability to share thoughts and knowledge, recognizing how valuable they are.

INSIGHTS INTO LEARNING AND TEACHING

Kim: I was coming into this partnership having taught in engineering for 15 years. Engineers value quantitative, clearly defined expectations. One of the many valuable things that you brought to the partnership was your background in the humanities. The proposed course that we were working on was designed for engineers, but really had humanities content. We spent quite a lot of time navigating the tensions between these two perspectives in determining how to structure activities and assessments. Given that the course audience was engineering students who had little non-technical writing background, how much could we or should we expect from them?

Amarachi: This part was one of the more challenging sections to think through because we had different expectations of a learning environment. In my program, I was used to discussion as primary practice in engaging with materials in lectures, and it never occurred to me the unease and difficulty that might arise for students who rarely engaged in this way until you raised that concern. This allowed us to be intentional in crafting a space to encourage meaningful dialogue.

Kim: Just as we had to build trust to make our partnership work, I will have to build trust with my students to facilitate open, honest discussion. The topics we will tackle are often difficult, potentially divisive issues. My classroom experience in this was limited to teaching about harassment and discrimination in the workplace. There, I found that framing harassment discussions so that the students were considering themselves as managers who had to deal with a complaint was more effective than considering themselves as potential perpetrators. The students could (and hopefully will) not all share one perspective.

Amarachi: My experiences with past courses and approaches my own instructors took to build safe spaces helped in trying to create an open class environment. The recognition of the ways in which identities informed our views and the myriad of views that students would bring into the conversation meant we had to think about how to deal with inevitable tensions in conversation and ensuring boundaries were created to allow for open and respectful dialogue. We talked about calling people in, rather than calling them out, and outlining community rules of engagement from the beginning of the course, which I think was necessary and informed by our discussion on the privilege and fragility sections.

Kim: The course content informed the mode of delivery.

Amarachi: Fragility and privilege informed our approaches to discussing structural resistance in the engineering field but also to course delivery and the resistance that would most likely emerge there. I think our discussions around the potential resistance from students with privileged identities was informed by our own experiences engaging in these conversations, which allowed us to pre-emptively strategize on ways to include allies alongside underrepresented students, without recentering those who are privileged.

Kim: It was interesting to see how a course developed in conversation would also use conversation as one of the key mechanisms of creating knowledge. I was initially uncomfortable with subjective forms of assessment, and I wasn't sure how to effectively motivate in-class discussions (which were clearly essential) and whether I should link them directly to assessments.

It was helpful to share my knowledge on constructive alignment in course design. We had to ensure that our learning objectives for the course were closely linked to the activities and to the assessments. That led to some interesting discussions about the learning objectives themselves. When we first considered them, we focused on course content, and it was helpful to consider what skills the students should have by the end of the course.

Amarachi: Having no experience in course design, I sometimes found it challenging to consider how the different aspects of the course all informed each other. I was always aware of the overarching goal of the course but was not always thinking about the ways each activity, discussion question, assessment, and even the topic order had to be intentionally aligned.

Kim: I think we both appreciated that there was a social agenda guiding the course. This clear purpose (equipping our students to build more equitable work environments) helped guide us. Answers to our "how do we?" questions were answered by "why are we?"

Amarachi: Yeah, the purpose of the course is why I'm so excited to see how the course will go! I can't wait to possibly come sit in for a lecture!

ADVICE FOR STUDENTS AND PROFESSORS IN PARTNERSHIP

1. Leave space for conversation, trust building, and vulnerability. While it may sometimes feel like conversation is not efficient, we found it was essential in developing an equitable partnership. We also developed insights together that we would not have achieved on our own.
2. Establish a strong shared purpose very early and maintain some structure. A clear vision always helps motivation, while the structure ensures productivity while scaffolding the student partner's transition from knowledge consumer to knowledge producer.
3. Strive for interdisciplinarity. It disrupts existing power dynamics and allows real learning from different perspectives on teaching and learning.

We were so grateful for the opportunity to partner in the creation of this course. Through conversation, we both learned and grew, and benefited from one another's disciplinary expertise. Despite our different roles and backgrounds, prioritizing open conversation ensured we had a productive and truly equitable partnership.

Chapter Three

A Medical Humanities Curriculum in Medical School

Unexpected Partnerships and Unintended Consequences

Julie Chen and John Ho

CONTEXT

The Medical Humanities (MH) curriculum is a compulsory part of the Bachelor of Medicine, Bachelor of Surgery (MBBS) program at the University of Hong Kong, a research-intensive university that admits 265 medical students per year to its over 30,000 strong student body. During the 2012 reform of undergraduate medical education, MH was proposed as a means through which doctors working in technologically advanced, difficult, and emotionally charged conditions can learn to be more humanistic and toward both their patients and themselves. It now encompasses about 100 hours of face-to-face learning spanning all 6 years of study for all 1,400+ currently enrolled medical students and has involved over 110 teachers who are a mix of clinicians, scientists, humanities or social sciences scholars, and arts educators/practitioners.

The MH curriculum is a work-in-progress and its iterative approach is highly dependent on the partnership with students. Students were involved in the initial consultative process of curriculum development and throughout the progressive roll-out of the curriculum to present. For example, as members of the initial staff-student MH planning group their ideas helped to shape the curriculum, and as contributors of original work for teaching material or as peer-tutors leading a workshop, they have helped to co-create learning. Some students were particularly inspired to engage because they truly believed in the goals of the curriculum. Julie Chen is an academic staff member who led the development of the MH curriculum from the outset, and John Ho is one of those engaged students, with brilliant and brave ideas, who was encouraging and persistent, and who was not afraid to do the work. This is the story of our pedagogical partnership over the past six years and how it transcended the curriculum to influence the broader learning culture.

WHO WE ARE AND WHY WE CHOSE TO
WORK IN PARTNERSHIP

Julie: I am Julie Chen, a family physician and medical educator, appointed as Associate Professor (Teaching) and Chief, Undergraduate Education in the Department of Family Medicine and Primary Care. While my main teaching responsibilities lie in family medicine, my teaching philosophy focuses on humanism and professionalism. These are the attributes beyond clinical competence that are integral to good doctoring and that I would like to see nurtured in our future doctors. In addition, in my role as Assistant Dean (Learner Wellbeing), I am responsible for overseeing the support of student mental and emotional wellbeing. As such, humanism, professionalism, wellbeing are all concepts that underpin and inspire my approach to teaching, the areas of the curriculum that I have helped to develop and the focus of my scholarship and research in teaching and learning. I co-developed the Medical Humanities curriculum that launched in 2012, and I continue to coordinate and teach in it.

John: I am John Ho, a final year medical student and a zealous contributor of numerous projects and initiatives within and outside the faculty during my six years of studentship. Medicine is my second career (I was previously an investment banker), and HKUMed is my second home. I circled back "home" after an elaborate detour. Matured and enriched by years of multinational, multidisciplinary experience and exposure, I embarked on my journey in medicine with a dedication to serve our future patients, colleagues, healthcare system, and community with a humble and humanistic heart. Viewing our "family matters" with a fresh pair of eyes, I have over the years proposed and worked with the faculty on visions ranging from curriculum, infrastructure, logistics to culture that have positively transformed our community experience. My passion hinges on this relentless belief that the student body forms an integral part of tertiary education, from which sprouts great ideas and that gives birth to future leaders, and therefore, hope for our society and humanity. The way our students are nurtured today will become a pattern through their professional careers, as they rise to become our future leaders. We must therefore strive to create a nurturing culture and environment, empowering each of them to thrive as a well-rounded person and a competent and dedicated health professional.

Julie: Our partnership was somewhat unusual as it was not an active decision to work together, but rather a fortuitous series of intersecting encounters in the Medical Humanities curriculum from the first to final year of John's medical studies. This opportunity for long-term interaction helped to build the trust and mutual understanding of our individual interests, character, and values that led to the goal of the partnership. In essence, this was to extend the vision of the MH curriculum "to deepen the experience of being human, to cultivate humaneness, to be a humanitarian" into the reality of medical school life.

John: Our partnership was unintentional, born out of a teacher-student relationship with mutual trust and respect that took years to develop. Dr. Chen first impressed me as someone with many respectable qualities: very friendly, caring toward student matters, down-to-earth, energetic, hardworking, passionate for teaching, radiating a great deal of positivity, humble, and receptive toward new ideas and suggestions. We crossed paths again over the next couple of years for different reasons. We spoke on a similar wavelength and had many core values in common. Trust was gradually built through dialogues and mutual understanding, as we conversed in the search for articulation and assimilation of great ideals of medical humanities in our curriculum, culture, and daily practice.

HOW OUR PARTNERSHIP EVOLVED: CRITICAL INCIDENTS AND CRITICAL INSIGHTS

Julie: There were three key incidents that underpinned our pedagogical partnership. I recall meeting John at the end of his first year of study when he requested to meet in order to give feedback on the first year MH curriculum. While he was very diplomatic in pointing out the strengths of the curriculum, he was much more passionate when he drew on his personal experience to advocate for a curriculum that focused more on 'practical medical humanities.' These were the interpersonal and communication skills needed to provide humane and empathetic care to patients. The medical curriculum already had a separate clinical interpersonal skills program that he would undertake in the coming years, but the experiential nature of his suggestion and the link of medical humanities to the real lives of medical students resonated.

John: The Medical Humanities curriculum in junior years back then put more emphasis on self-exploration through which we took the avenues of music, art, movies, books, plays, meditation, exercises, and other means for such reflection. MH contrasted vividly the otherwise highly vocational, practical, no-frills, core medical curriculum. It was initially challenging for many of my peers to appreciate the beauty of the essence of the MH curriculum as

they struggled to grasp its relevance in their current studies and future practice. Reality was cruel in our warzone-like hospitals here in the city. There
was plenty of room to tailor our MH curriculum, bringing it closer to practical reality without sacrificing its spirit of self-discovery, addressing antici-
pated challenges through building early resilience in our cohort. I had faith
that Dr. Chen would be receptive toward constructive suggestions, so I
reached out and asked for a meeting to go over concerns and ideas.

Julie: The fourth year MH curriculum sought to explore the personal
experiences of loss, healing, and survivorship, and one of the assignments
was the submission of an annotated original photo that reflects the human
experience of suffering and healing, whether happy scenes of patients in
recovery, or evidence of challenges faced by patients during their illness. Our
second encounter was through this assignment, which was a very personal
sharing from John that I saw as a teacher, but affected me as a human being.
This was medical humanities linking to real life and having an impact.

John: My mother passed away right at the beginning of my clinical studies. I was in and out of hospitals every day for several months as she battled
the last moments. I was shattered, even doubted my path to medicine, when
all I witnessed was the apparent nothing that could be done to save her from
the slow death and suffering. In tears I wrote my mother a public letter in
remembrance of her and submitted the same piece of writing with the last
photo I took with her in hospital for the MH assignment. It was medical
humanities in blood and tears, trumping all intellectual understanding of MH
philosophies, as it cut through the deepest wound that would only heal from
the sharpest pain. Even to this day I am still grateful that Dr. Chen reached
out to care for me the moment she read my piece; that was the time I felt
most vulnerable.

Julie: The final year MH curriculum comprises a number of small group
tutorials focusing on "staying human, maintaining professionalism and building resilience." Led by a clinician, students reflect on their clinical experiences to date: the good, the bad, and the ugly. The groups have spoken about
the culture and hierarchy on the hospital wards, moral dilemmas encountered, bullying and harassment, but also gratitude to the patients for allowing
them to be part of their lives, the joy of small successes and first experiences,
and the camaraderie and bonding among classmates and peers. This structured learning opportunity built into the MH curriculum led to the watershed
incident: a series of discussions that John and I had, precipitated by a group
discussion during an MH tutorial about experiencing disrespectful behaviors
in the learning environment that were undermining morale and discouraging
effective learning. This unfortunate reality of medical school was something
we wanted to change.

John: It has somewhat been an unwritten public secret for decades con-
cerning the practice of paternalistic, occasionally unwelcoming or even hos-

tile culture. Traditional Asian conservatism might have coerced many to stay silent over the years, internalizing fears through coping, accepting things as they were, or just having too little faith to believe that collectivism could possibly bring positive changes. It broke my heart listening to my peers' sharing. Their words accentuated my own experience and struck fear in me that the same pattern would replicate through generations until unfortunate things could happen at the most unpredictable time. The culture of bullying, deliberate hostility, and harassment amongst other moral dilemmas shared by my colleagues highlighted the necessity of having a structure, system, and formal executive-level endorsement that would safeguard not only learners' wellbeing in the long term but also core principles and values that defines this institution. Dr. Chen and I took the conversation through the hierarchy with proposals and references to publications, guidelines, and protocols from overseas institutions.

Julie: The discussions, background work, and advocacy that John and I undertook were timely as HKUMed was prioritizing the area of student wellbeing. As Assistant Dean (Learner Wellbeing), I thought it was important to start by determining the core principles that underpin a learning environment and culture that allow learners to thrive, to fully engage in the learning process, and to reach their full potential. Articulating these agreed-upon core principles would make visible the standard we wished to uphold. Our work together, supported by the contributions of many other students, colleagues, and the Faculty Teaching and Learning leadership team, led to the eventual creation, endorsement, publication, and wide dissemination of a statement of agreed principles toward a respectful learning culture and a teaching and learning charter by and for members of the HKUMed educational community. This was a gratifying but unintended consequence of the MH curriculum. This was MH in action, a step toward fulfilling that aspect of the MH vision, "to cultivate humaneness," by extending it beyond discussion and debriefing in the MH tutorial and bringing it into the wider learning sphere.

INSIGHTS GAINED ABOUT WORKING IN PARTNERSHIP

Julie: From this experience, I found that a successful pedagogical partnership need not follow a set model or prescribed structure, but can be fluid in content and process. Contributions to the partnership can be any or all of these: ideas, information, contacts, learning materials, face-to-face teaching etc. The partnership may involve regular or ad hoc interactions, be formal or informal, project-based or open-ended, deliberate or unpredictable. It doesn't even have to be called a partnership. More important are the elements of a partnership: the beliefs and values that coalesce into a common vision, a commitment to making it happen, and trust. It took almost five years of getting to know each other through formal teaching sessions, in-person meetings about different interests, lengthy emails, and more than a little serendipity, to bring us together and for this partnership to find its purpose. This was time well spent and necessary as it gave us the foundational trust to move forward.

John: There should be no rule book to pedagogical partnership.That said, there are key principles underlying a conducive environment for constructing one. I would call it "Relational Activism," an approach through which a directional objective is attained through relationship-based reiteration. Visualize the concept as a circular chain with three elements: trust-based relationship, common objective, and iterative actions. Join them head to toe as they come in full circle. Educators or students can construct a pedagogical partnership at any point of the circle: building relationships through daily interactions, drawn together through working toward a common goal, idea, or pursuit, or participate in Special Interest Groups as ideas take flight in the iterative action phase. Pedagogical partnership can take any form and size, as long as the group moves toward a common grand finale.

INSIGHTS INTO LEARNING AND TEACHING

Julie: Upon reflecting on our experience, I am much more cognizant of the interrelationship between formal curricular initiatives and the learning environment, culture, or social setting in which students are immersed. I am also much more aware of the hidden curriculum, those unwritten norms and taken-for-granted practices that are absorbed by immersion in a learning culture. After hearing of specific distressing examples from student experience, I am even more concerned about the significant impact it can have. The hidden curriculum can undermine the intended goals of the formal curriculum when it is allowed to fester, but when recognized and used as source material for teaching and learning, it can also be a powerful tool to promote change. As a direct curricular outcome of our partnership work, MH tutorial tutors are guided to explicitly address student mistreatment in the learning environment, a topic that is now raised in the Professionalism in Practice program of the medical curriculum, in which scenarios based on real-life situations are triggers for exploring unprofessional behavior.

John: Education should be a bidirectional interactive experience, far from a didactic dogmatic approach, although the latter has long been the accepted norm in this part of the world. Particularly true for humanities subjects that have no hard-and-fast rule regarding right and wrong, pedagogical partnership encourages mutual ownership and active contribution. With a shared common objective under the umbrella of mutual trust and respect, both teachers and students are constantly prompted to critically analyze the merits of their own arguments, judgments, and blind spots. Through vigorous discussions, even constructive debates, and eventual compromise and action, pedagogical partnership through relational activism has a high propensity of achieving satisfactory and sustainable changes and learning outcomes.

ADVICE FOR OTHERS

First, be brave. Brave in trying something new, for a new purpose, with someone new. Neither of us knew where our partnership initiative would lead or how it would be received. We ventured into that 'brave space' introduced by the editors of this book, as we needed to be frank but respectful in discussing first-hand, sensitive issues that could have direct and real implications for students and teachers. Simultaneously, we challenged each other by examining ideas that are unpopular, politically sensitive, or difficult to implement. Be bold and honest; do not be afraid of challenging dogma; embrace the uncomfortable conversation; feel the fear, yet for good causes and righteousness move forward with confidence and humility. Leaders take the road less traveled, so take it.

Second, recognize that partnerships are out there, just waiting for a cause. Fundamentally, students and teachers in an institution are already striving for the same thing: to make university education truly worthwhile. While the world may seem to be increasingly self-absorbed and pragmatic, our experience has shown that we can make time and prioritize work that has meaning. Students do need to achieve the grades to pass the year and teachers do need to make tenure and retain their jobs, but students will set aside their quest for grades, and teachers will set aside their pursuit of grants and publications, when there is a cause, project, or initiative that they believe in. Be present in the moment, make yourself available, open up your mind for possibilities, promote your creativity and passion. Other change-makers are out there, so just look.

Last, but never the least, our advice is to do everything in Love, in the broadest sense. Guard hearts, intention, and deeds during the course of the partnership. Be completely humble and gentle, be patient and bear with one another in respect and understanding. Agree to disagree, for the partnership calls upon ideals that are greater than the people themselves. Against any odds, however challenging it might seem during the process, love and righteousness will prevail in the end. Do not be discouraged, stand firm on truth, care for others the way we long to be cared for. Have faith in one another, stay hopeful when challenges loom, and after all wrap everything we do in Love.

Chapter Four

Peers and Colleagues

*Collaborative Class Design through
Student-Faculty Partnerships*

Angela Gennocro and John Straussberger

CONTEXT

Provided by Bill Reynolds, Director of the Lucas Center for Faculty Development.

The Student-Faculty Partnership Program (SFPP) at Florida Gulf Coast University is a joint faculty development and student success initiative. It began in the fall of 2018 as a collaboration between the staff and faculty of the Lucas Center for Faculty Development and the FGCU Dean of Students office, and the program receives funding from the Division of Academic Affairs. The SFPP is modeled after the Students as Leaders and Teachers (SaLT) program at Bryn Mawr College, and Alison Cook-Sather, who facilitates SaLT, has been a consultant to FGCU's partnership program since its inception.

The SFPP pairs college faculty members with undergraduate students who assume the role of paid teaching consultant to their faculty partners. These pairs collaborate for an entire semester to enrich teaching and learning in a particular course. Students observe their faculty partners' classes once a week, take detailed observation notes, and meet weekly to discuss their observations and offer feedback about teaching and learning. In addition, faculty and student groups meet separately at regular intervals to share information and support one another. In the first three semesters of the program 24 students participated and, of these, 11 were partners in two or more semesters. In addition, 33 faculty and one administrator have participated, and one of those faculty members participated twice.

INTRODUCTION

When first starting to teach, faculty are often encouraged to create a clear barrier between themselves and their students, with the implicit advice being that this will help establish authority and facilitate classroom management. This, at least, was John's experience in graduate school, when new teaching assistants gathered for a brief orientation before taking over recitations and grading for what were usually very large lecture courses. At the time, this advice made sense to John; establishing a classroom hierarchy while still opening a space for dialogue is a daunting task for young teachers. Teaching assistants were warned against being perceived as peers to their students, and thereby losing the ability to enforce policies or hand back less-than-stellar grades. They were also warned against being passive to the point of being either barely tolerated by students, or at worst completely ignored. While this approach imposed "order," it also created a clear divide between faculty and students, leading some students to be hesitant to ask for help, for instance, or some faculty members to dismiss well-founded student feedback as simply "complaining."

This chapter explores alternative models for student-faculty interactions that focus on peer exchange and eventually collaboration. More specifically, it charts the emergence of classroom co-production between two members of the pilot cohort of the Student-Faculty Partnership Program at Florida Gulf Coast University in Fall 2018. The particular partnership at the center of this chapter was between Angela Gennocro, a fourth-year biology major and management minor, and John Straussberger, a second-year Assistant Professor of African History at the time. The two of us collaborated on a general education history course entitled "World Civilization since 1815," which was comprised of students from a wide range of academic disciplines, years of study, and skill levels. The goal of this and the other student-faculty partnerships in Florida Gulf Coast University's program was to increase engagement by incorporating students' perspectives into classroom management and course design.

Embracing partnerships between faculty and students, in particular those that include collaboration and curricular co-creation, can build upon the benefits of previous approaches that formulate student partners as "consultants." Students who actively participate in the production of research and curriculum "reveal spaces of agency, knowledge, and solidarity" that lead to reinvention of both classrooms and the larger university (Steffen 2017, 20). The narrative that follows charts one such example of a student-faculty partnership developing into collaboration through both its initial challenges and ultimate success. In particular, it follows how a student observation early in the semester led to open discussion of classroom dynamics, possible solutions, and eventually the development of a new classroom activity that responded to the initial questions. This example points to the ways in which student-faculty partnerships can facilitate increased responsiveness to student perspectives and classroom dynamics. Student-faculty partnerships also include a large amount of labor, and while the benefits to the faculty member are obvious, for the student they are less so. By pointing to an example where a student interested in a career in education took an active role in curriculum design, the narrative below underscores the perspective that effective partnerships further the development of faculty and student partners alike.

MOTIVATION FOR ENGAGING IN PARTNERSHIP

Angela: As a student partner with the aspirations of becoming a secondary school educator, I wanted to gain experience in the classroom, which a strictly STEM undergraduate degree did not provide. Once I discovered the Student-Faculty Partnership Program (SFPP), I began to envision teaching in my own classroom in a few years. I knew that by participating in a pedagogical partnership at the postsecondary level, I would enhance my understanding of the learning process and curriculum development at other levels of study. I also had the desire to find out what typical academic struggles were for college students so that I could address some of those issues in my prospective secondary classrooms. I was eager to gain insight from a professor as to how I could navigate those challenges, as well as establish an ongoing relationship with a faculty member for potential professional connections or opportunities in the future.

John: The key catalyst for engaging in the partnership, from my perspective, was to incorporate more thorough, thoughtful, and substantive feedback on a recurring general education course: the end goal being improving student engagement and comprehension. I had grown increasingly unsatisfied with the standard model of feedback used at the university—for example, anonymous student evaluations conducted at the end of the course—and wanted a more productive model for addressing student concerns and viewpoints. The SFPP model seemed to address many of the reservations I had with the previous framework. It also provided the extra benefit of building collaboration with a partner who would have in-depth, extensive knowledge about the course design and classroom setting. There were several challenges to overcome, though. The SFPP was a significant investment in time and thought, one that, if it was going to be successful, would require sustained effort over the course of the semester and a certain amount of flexibility.

Angela and I would also have to bridge the traditional student-faculty divide, and I would have to actively counter the sometimes-reflexive dismissal of student concerns. The biggest challenge for me, though, was overcoming the potentially awkward or uncomfortable experience of receiving constant critique of my teaching style and class design. However, I believed the benefits of the partnership outweighed the challenges.

ORIGINATION AND DEVELOPMENT OF PARTNERSHIP

We think one of the key breakthroughs of the partnership occurred early in the process. Namely, to overcome that challenge of ingrained biases and power differentials, as well as the reticence to offer and receive what could be critical feedback, we needed to establish a peer relationship based upon mutual respect. To establish this trusting relationship, we spent considerable time in many of the early meetings, while going over the notes produced as a result of the classroom observations, *feeling out* the personality and approach of the other partner. The SFPP coordinators stressed that this process included understanding the background and perspective of each partner—John, for instance, highlighted his experience as a returned Peace Corps volunteer, and Angela talked about her interest in teaching and biology—in order to better understand one another. We also needed to develop what the goals of the partnership would be, and agree on an approach that would best realize those intended outcomes. Our answers to these key questions evolved over time, and required adaptation on both of our parts. What resulted was a partnership that built upon consultation to embrace collaboration. In essence, we would work together to improve components of the course, and the product that resulted was co-constructed.

Angela: Since the preliminary stages of the partnership, John and I wanted the focus of the semester to be the development of the course for current and future students. We agreed that the cornerstone of the program was to enrich the learning experience for students. As such, I did not want to act as a Teaching Assistant, or a liaison between students and John when issues were to arise. Instead, my role was to observe the dynamics of the classroom, such as how John delivered content to students, or which students were more responsive at various points throughout the semester. Following observations, I would send John a typed report including my account of classroom observations, alongside my descriptions and questions stemming from those observations.

During some of the earlier observations, I was able to identify some of John's practices that resulted in either agreeable or indifferent responses from the students, and other practices that I thought of as exceedingly well thought-out and deserving of recognition. As the semester progressed, I was able to generate recommendations for John to consider. Both John and I understood that not all of my recommendations or suggestions would be put into practice in the classroom, or in lesson planning; they were tools for guidance that could be implemented at John's discretion.

Further into our partnership, John's routine practice became familiar to me, and I was struggling to make novel recommendations that we had not discussed in the partnership before. Both John and I agreed that a new dimension of the partnership could be added: I would develop and execute a lesson for the course with John's guidance at each stage of the process. This proposed activity sought to address an observation I had made earlier in the semester, that John, not the students, offered most discussion questions that pushed students to analyze difficult texts or concepts. I suggested that an improvement would include having students ask these types of questions to one another. Although I did not have expertise regarding the historical topic, as my area of study is science, John wanted to allow me the opportunity to grasp a different perspective through the partnership. In addition to this, he wanted to allow me a chance to gain firsthand experience with instruction in a classroom. The ultimate goal was to provide an engaging educational experience for the current students in the course, as well as future students that both of us would teach in the future.

At this point, the partnership evolved from an observation-consultation dynamic to a co-construction relationship. We agreed on when the classroom activity would take place and at which points I would provide my ideas for the classroom activity to John in our meetings prior to the activity. So that I could gain an understanding of what the context of the activity should be, John also provided me with articles that pertained to the course material and the readings the students were expected to complete for the particular class.

In the following weeks, I provided John with a few ideas for classroom activities that could be further developed. We came to a consensus as to which activity would be the most fruitful for the students, as well as most relevant to the readings that they would be completing. John provided me with ideas as to how the activity could be enhanced, such as taking advantage of the expo markers and dry erase boards around the classroom and recommending smaller group sizes for the activity. Once we discussed all of our ideas for the activity, we completed a written proposal for the activity.

On the day of the class activity, I acted as the class facilitator. I explained the instructions for the activity, divided students into groups, and was available to students as they asked questions pertaining to the activity. John was available to students to answer questions that pertained to the course content. Students were engaged in the activity and select students showcased and explained their work at the end of the class.

Following the activity, John and I met to discuss its strengths and weaknesses. John gave praise and recommendations, and I was able to walk away from the partnership with constructive critiques for when I am an educator myself. Our roles as partners had been reversed, which in turn provided an in-depth experience of the partnership and a mutually beneficial experience for all parties involved.

John: The idea for Angela to develop an activity emerged organically from a partnership that in many ways set the stage for more in-depth collaboration. We had established a pattern of taking suggestions that Angela made about the course—providing an outline for a lecture on the first slide of the presentation, for instance, or managing students who were distracted and in doing so distracted others—putting them into place, observing the effects they had, and then developing and implementing additional modifications in response. This iterative process provided a real-time feedback mechanism, rather than my having to wait for the end of the course and hoping to implement changes in the next semester. The development of a class exercise by Angela herself was a formalization of this already existing process that had been developed earlier in the semester.

Angela developing an exercise also addressed one of the concerns I had with the partnership: namely, I was receiving almost all of the benefit from Angela's extensive work. While the program did provide a stipend, the compensation did not reflect the value of her labor. Partnerships work best when both parties are invested in and benefit from the project. Therefore, we would have to work out a way that furthered Angela's own goals and interests. Angela had previously expressed interest in entering the teaching profession. This partnership seemed to be an ideal setting where Angela could be introduced to teaching while also making use of my background in the profession. The exercise we developed—and more broadly the partnership as a whole—benefited greatly from collaboration and co-construction. I ended up with changes to the course that I will continue to implement going forward, and Angela was able to gain early insight into course design and class management.

INSIGHT GAINED ABOUT WORKING IN PARTNERSHIP

We think that faculty and student partners approaching one another as peers and collaborators is essential to a successful outcome. Having mutual respect and valuing the different perspectives of each partner allow for a dynamic evaluation of existing practices and frameworks. Working in partnerships requires the combined effort of both parties involved, not just one member of the partnership should be the sole contributor. Being flexible with one another regarding deadlines and meeting times when personal circumstances may remove a partner from their work for a set time is also important and may even result in a stronger collaboration on a professional level.

The SFPP also introduced a destabilizing element to what could have been a stale course, allowing for productive reevaluation and adaptation. Either out of necessity or complacency, teachers fall into routines, especially in courses that are taught every semester. Introducing a fresh and critical viewpoint into the classroom—especially one from a student—opened up a space where areas for growth could be identified, new exercises and techniques developed, and old ideas rethought while at the same time underscoring what was already working. Finally, and most importantly, the partnership also gave us new perspectives on teaching and learning, leading to durable transformations in the way that we approached our work.

Angela: By working in a partnership program such as this one, I had to step out of my comfort zone when having to give constructive criticism to John. At first, I was unsure how the messages would be perceived, but I knew that he was participating in the partnership for his own personal development, as well as the betterment of the educational process of his students. I had to learn how to deliver messages to John in a practical yet encouraging way.

I also gained a much greater appreciation for the teaching process, in particular the work that goes into planning, organizing, and delivering a lesson in an effective and meaningful way. There is a preconceived notion that since most professors are experts in their respective disciplines, they do not need to prepare much for their course lectures prior to delivering them. After working through the partnership, I came to realize that this idea could not be further from the truth. Professors put immense amounts of time into their lectures, planning activities that will allow students to gain transferable skills that they can carry beyond the classroom, and doing additional research on their subjects so they can further their own understanding of the content they are teaching so they can better instruct their students.

John: The partnership also had effects on my pedagogy that extended beyond the specific course on which we collaborated. In explaining my own rationale for assignments, activities, or practices in the course while talking with Angela, I came to realize the extensive benefits of transparency. Why I am doing particular things in class can be opaque to students, especially when I assume that they will implicitly understand the value of a specific writing exercise or group discussion. Explicitly stating my rationale behind a particular decision or design to students allows them to see the course as not something that is dictated to them from *on high*, but rather a thoughtful plan to develop content knowledge, as well as skills that can be extended beyond the confines of the particular course. Since working with Angela, I have attempted to include more pedagogical transparency with students. I explain my rationale behind the meta-structure of the course as well as individual assignments, and the content- and skill-specific goals I hope students gain.

Just as importantly, I am also much more open to student input and suggestions while the course is unfolding. All too often, faculty dismiss student perspectives. And indeed, some student comments are simply complaints about having to put effort into learning. In this manner, Angela was a very useful resource for identifying which comments had merit and which could be dismissed. Yet students have important insights into their own learning, and teachers should be responsive to insights that students can provide. I tell students that if they can make a compelling case for a change in the course, then I am open to making changes. This resulted from the mutual respect developed during the partnership, which encouraged me to understand more clearly the perspective of students.

ADVICE FOR THOSE PARTAKING IN PARTNERSHIP

For those who are interested in participating in partnerships such as this one, it is crucial to be sensitive to feedback, whether it is being given or received. Mutual respect is the key to a successful partnership. For faculty, this means listening to the feedback provided by the student partner, and implementing suggested changes. For both partners, it means collaborating on building an adapted course structure and classroom environment and sometimes swallowing one's pride to an extent, and opening oneself up to giving and receiving critique.

The essential goal of this partnership is student and staff development on the individual and collective levels for the current time, as well as for times to come. A perspective that is greater than oneself must be attained in order to further the enhancement of others. Whether the results can be seen by the partners or not is irrelevant to the work that must be put forth. The work conducted via this type of partnership may influence people later on without the initial contributors having any idea that their contribution made an impact. Putting work in for the betterment of others, rather than receiving validation or congratulations is the mindset one must have when participating in any stage of a pedagogical partnership.

As previously stated, the SFPP requires a significant amount of time and contemplation. We believe that to make the most of this investment, one has to approach the other partner as not just a consultant or client, but as a collaborator, someone who co-constructs the course. This relationship model provides a more dynamic setting while also leveraging the strengths of the student and faculty partners.

REFERENCE

Steffen, H. (2017). Inventing our university: Student-faculty collaboration in critical university studies. *Radical Teacher, 108*, 19–27.

Chapter Five

Voicing and Reflecting in a Pedagogical Partnership

Doron Narkiss and Iska Naaman

Kaye Academic College in Beer Sheva, Israel, trains preservice teachers for all compulsory school subjects. The authors of this chapter, Dr. Doron Narkiss and Ms. Iska Naaman, lecture and study there, respectively. Doron lectures on literature in the Department of English. At the time of the partnership, Iska was a third-year student (of four), a preservice trainee in Bible Studies and Hebrew Literature. For the project, Iska attended the first semester of Doron's year-long Introduction to Fiction course, a basic introductory course in the English department.

WHY WE JOINED THE PARTNERSHIP

Iska: When the College published a call for second- and third-year students to join a pilot partnership project, I registered at once. I spoke with the student who told us about the program, and as I received more details I became more and more interested. Later there were personal interviews at the College where more information was given about the project in general, about the source of the idea, the vision, and what I was expected to do. I liked the idea that students would be given an opportunity to include their voices, offer opinions, and work towards influencing change. The project presented an innovative and bold vision, which I had not heard of before; I immediately wanted to participate as one of the innovators. Another benefit I saw in the program was attending an extra course, which would not give me a credit but would enrich my knowledge. I could then transfer that knowledge to the courses I was studying. Above all, the program requirements were clear and understandable, and I was quite sure I could fit them into my schedule.

The one-semester pilot project was constructed around three weekly meetings: observing the lesson in class; talking with the lecturer about the lesson; and a meeting of the observing students with the coordinator of the project, Dr. Ruthy Mansur Shahor. At our weekly meetings with Dr. Mansour Shahor, she reassured us and answered all our concerns. She showed us many ways to ask the lecturer questions about the lesson, and explained to us that our group was a "growth and development group." We worked with an observation page to assist us to focus on the pedagogical practice of the lecturer. In the meetings we learned about types of communication, and that we must work and meet with the lecturer for the "supporting discourse" type of communication. At each session, we reviewed the events that occurred in the classes and were shared by the students, so that we could look at concepts that emerged during the session in the following lessons.

I saw the importance and necessity of the project in several ways. I would be the students' voice and could tell the lecturer what I see, which might lead to change, or might require no change. The project can cause a conceptual shift in the lecturer's thought, as they listen to mature students who can be partners in analyzing and planning for teaching. This dynamic can develop the pedagogical professionalism of the chosen student. As a teacher to be, I get ideas from my lecturers and from their teaching methods, and implement them in my own classes. It can also teach the student how to be critical in a constructive way. To be an effective observer and pedagogical partner, a student must have a certain measure of maturity and responsibility to respond worthily to the lecturer's invitation into his classroom. Moreover, it is very important that the lecturer and the student be from different departments, to neutralize as far as possible the hierarchic relations between them. A student who does not depend on the lecturer for a grade, or for continuing studies, can potentially feel more able to tell the lecturer the whole truth.

Doron: It all began by mistake. In the run-up to the 2018/19 academic year, Prof. Leah Kozminsky, the president of the college, sent out a call to the faculty to participate in a faculty-student pedagogical partnership program. Around the same time, she and I happened to discuss the possibility of opening a student-faculty internet-based journal. When I received the invitation for the former, I assumed it was the latter issue I had been invited for, and so I was not surprised to see students as well as faculty in the meeting room. I did not initially understand what was being projected, and when told, felt cold fear grip my heart (I was reading a lot of Poe at the time). However, Kaye College has a reputation for and a history of developing and adapting innovative educational practices, and this was not the first project I had participated in, and benefitted from (granted, I was usually more aware of what I was getting into at the outset). Moreover, my trust in Prof. Kozminsky's academic and pedagogical expertise convinced me to suspend judgment, in other words not to bolt at once. In the time between realizing the purpose of the meeting and signing on irrevocably with a completely un-known person to observe my classes—a student no less—I reviewed to my-self all the possibilities of observation that I had hitherto avoided.

The idea of this particular type of student-faculty partnership was new to me. I know peer review—a colleague from the field or the department does you a favor and sits in on one lesson and then gives feedback; preservice and new teachers suffer for tenure review; a Ministry inspector calls; the princi-pal has to fill in a report. They all sound about as appealing as a dentist's appointment. I recalled Simon and Boyer's (1967–1974) multi-volume work on the 99 systems of observation, *Mirrors for Behavior*, with a shudder. I have considered using another method—videotaping, perhaps—and I do pe-ruse the student feedback at the end of every semester, but finally, observa-tion makes me uneasy, student feedback comes too late and is often contra-dictory, and watching myself perform on video is cringeworthy. Despite this, I have long wanted to receive an observer's reflection, to validate as well as improve my teaching.

If, as Wragg (2012 [1994], 3) suggests, "[t]he purpose, timing and context of an observation should largely determine its methods," then here, I per-suaded myself, the purpose was to inform the observed (me) on the quality of my work, over a relatively long period (a full semester, 13 ninety-minute lessons), in the context of a reciprocal relationship between the teacher and the observer. In other words, the observer (Iska) would learn about my teach-ing methods as I learned about my particular foibles as a teacher.

On consideration, then, a pedagogical partnership sounded like a more promising approach than others. If it is a truism that nobody knows what goes on in a classroom once the door has closed, except (perhaps) the teacher and the students, then it follows that the best situated respondents to the quality of a teacher's teaching are the students. Yet the students of a particu-lar course have to attain knowledge and are not available to support the lecturer by giving detailed feedback every lesson; nor could a lecturer as-sume that the response was not colored by extraneous concerns. But a student who was not studying in the course and was not there to receive a grade, whose sole reason for being in the class was to document and reflect what she saw, from a student's point of view, of the lecturer's interaction with the class—this could be a much less painful way of assessing my teaching and giving me an idea of how effective it was for the students' learning.

WORKING TOGETHER

Doron: Knowing that the observer in the partnership, Iska, was a student, placed her on the students' "side." These hierarchic gradations are impos-sible to avoid in academic settings. Knowing that she was there to observe my teaching and classroom strategies placed the project in a practical context for the students, and made it imperative for them that she should observe for them as well, and reflect their needs, as indeed she did. The very visibility of the project has additional value in modeling research or an innovative method for improving an individual's teaching. The project also models institutional support of, and commitment to, innovative educational practices. Iska's position placed her within, as a student, but also outside of the accepted hierarchy—making her a source of empowerment for the students, their "voice," as she calls it, and an agent for change; an intermediary between them and me; and an authority for me on the perception of my teaching, and ultimately on my students' learning, telling me what she calls "the whole truth."

I was wary of being observed by a student, worried that she would not appreciate my manner of teaching, the rationale behind it, and my aims. However, innovation including the student perspective cannot even be attempted where there is no dialogue, and it must be actively encouraged for students to become agents of change (Templeton, MacCracken & Smith, 2019). The personalities of the partners, and their agreement to share the highly personal subject of their own teaching and learning, are the best predictors of the success of such a partnership.

From the start, we were able to set up a meeting in the period following the course. We met nearly every week for half-an-hour to an hour. Iska had to separate the "subject" or "content knowledge" (of literary terms and analysis for example) from "teaching knowledge" (the formal procedure of acquainting learners with content [Shulman, 1986]). Her focus was on the latter, but of course the two intertwine, especially for Iska, who is training to become a literature teacher in school. Iska is a meticulous observer, and from the start, I gladly followed her lead in discussing the many points she brought up.

As our relationship developed and we came to trust each other's responses, I would occasionally discuss with Iska related situations in other classes, and consult with her, relying on her unique point of view, while she shared with me some of her teaching dilemmas, as well as her successes in her practice teaching in school. Part of my appreciation of Iska's thorough work in the partnership comes from knowing that she, like many other students in the College, is very busy. She is married with young children, and has a physically demanding job in addition to her compulsory hours studying at college and teaching at school. I find it admirable that despite this workload she volunteered to join the project. Moreover, her participation required her to observe a course held in English, which, although being a heritage language for her, is not her first language or one she uses often.

Iska is not unique in this. The student population at Kaye College in general is extremely diverse, and this must be taken into consideration in the implementation of a pedagogical partnership. Thus, many of the students are the first generation of their families to attend higher education, often with inappropriate expectations (Karp & Bork, 2014); many come from marginalized populations (Joldersma & Perhamus, 2020); very few have English as their mother tongue, indeed for many students in the English teacher-training department, where English is the medium of instruction, English is often their third or fourth language—and that this, the multiplicity of other languages and cultures and their felt presence, politicizes and historicizes, complicates and enriches teaching at the College (Napolitan & Bowman, 2018), as well as determining language teaching purposes, language level, and methods (see e.g. Mahboob, 2010; Medgyes, 1992; Moussu & Llurda, 2008; Vogel & García, 2017). As a department we have considered various ways to enhance student agency (Camangian, 2010; Assaf, Garza, & Battle, 2010; Fukada et al., 2017; Stanciu & Lin, 2017). These "institutional givens" were part of our shared understanding in the pedagogical partnership. Academically appropriate behavior is of structural importance. The fact of working together, despite our differences in age, experience, field, language, and culture, reveals a more equitable approach to teacher training, and finally to teaching itself, and engages a more critical approach for faculty and students to examine the terms of their teaching and learning—what is taught, to what purposes, and how (Cook-Sather & Felten, 2017).

Iska: As I said before, the project makes me the voice of the students; I become a partner in teaching and learning, and can advance my opinions and point of view; and, through close observation, the project also develops my pedagogical abilities. Doron has over thirty years of teaching experience and shows great confidence in class. The relationship between us was based on mutual respect, openness to one another, and cooperation. In our weekly meetings after the class, Doron would refer very seriously to my questions and comments. Thus, when I asked why he did not let students read the literary works aloud in class, but only read them himself, he shared his concern that the pronunciation and flow of the text might be less clear—but then from the very next lesson he decided to let the students read. His willingness to respect my feedback and implement timely change showed Doron's attentiveness to my questions, and his willingness to receive input from a student. In a similar collegial manner, Doron would reveal his rationale for his pedagogical outlook and the methodological actions he takes repeatedly in his teaching, from reading names at the beginning of each lesson (see Cook-Sather, 2019, on naming), to insisting on using printed copies of the works studied, to the actual choice of material and assessment techniques in the course.

One of the students who studied in the course also participated in the partnership with another lecturer in the project. She claimed in several meetings that she felt a change in Doron's teaching as a result of my presence in

class. She said that the material was taught at a slower pace, and she understood it better because Doron often repeated central ideas about the texts
being studied—but he did this from the start, so perhaps the change she felt
had another cause, such as her own growing involvement in the project, and
the perspectives on teaching and learning that it opened up for her.

WHAT WE LEARNED

Doron: The partnership provided insights into teaching and learning, which
can be divided into three broad, though connected, areas: the presence of a
student observer in class; my teaching; and the students' experience.

Iska's presence as an observer in the course for a semester made me more
self-aware about my teaching. This would probably have happened no matter
who the observer had been, but having a student in class subtly changed my
relationship to the students at the moment, and perhaps permanently. For the
first time, I had the possibility of gauging the effectiveness of what I taught
on the students' learning in real time, rather than in an essay or exam. It was
important that I put my best practices forward. Iska would reflect to me the
content I taught the class, that is, the material (Introduction to Fiction), as
well as reflecting my teaching practice to me. Her observer function made
me self-reflexively question my teaching practice not only in objective-seem-
ing terms of "getting the knowledge across" but in view of my position in the
pedagogical dialogue with a heterogeneous student population, a dialogue
which incorporates and reflects racial, cultural, and other differences between me and the students. Iska's student-as-observer function allowed me
access to the results of my own actions and reactions preparing, delivering,
and after the lesson. Metaphorically, Iska's reflections of and on my teaching
became my pedagogical compass, or conscience. For me, a thirty-year-plus
veteran of the classroom, our interactions returned a measure of humility to
my sense of myself in class, reminding me of the individuality of each
student and the uniqueness of each group, and of care and equity as critical
components of effective teaching (Howard, 2003).

The added awareness generated by being observed had an effect on my
teaching as well. The partnership provided me with agency to shift my view
from the imagined to the reasoned and actual. Even though my classroom
behavior is, I hope, quite communicative—discussing, listening, encouraging
dialogue—it is also quite structured, with goals and pace worked out in a
lesson plan in advance. The partnership extended my teaching repertoire,
making it more inclusive by spending more class time explaining, exemplifying, and ensuring understanding. The partnership was instrumental in leading
me to confront and reconsider not only the rationale of my pedagogical
practice (why do I read names in class, or do all the reading aloud?), but

more basically, the underlying assumptions of what it means to teach, to teach a particular group, to teach certain material and not other material, how to ensure learning, etc. No less important is the sense of revalidation: the project assured me that although there is, as always, room for improvement, there is also much that has stood the tests of time and changing audiences.

The student experience is an important part of the partnerships, but one I have little first-hand knowledge of. We both noted that Iska, in my course, and perhaps other student-observers in other courses, felt they were representing the students studying the course to some extent. This agency, coupled with a direct, one-on-one dialogue with a lecturer on his pedagogical practice creates a sense of responsibility, motivation, receptiveness, and critical appreciation of the teacher's role, and in the case of a student in a teacher-training college, of her own practice in years to come.

One of the students in the department whom I have been teaching for three years, and who participated in the pedagogical partnership with a lecturer outside the department, showed this pattern in her interactions with me. I find that the partnership has made her more confident and more able to imagine herself as a teacher in the near future.

For the other students in the class, I believe the partnership was beneficial as well. Not only did they have a representative to voice their needs, in me they could see a model of a veteran teacher willing to be observed, and implicitly willing to accept criticism of his pedagogical practice. This creates a flipped hierarchy: they are used to being observed by their seniors, whereas here the student observed and critiqued the lecturer. This may lead to independently conceived critiques of what and how they are being taught, and to their taking more responsibility for their own learning, as well as enabling them to be more accepting of critiques of their own pre- or in-service practice.

Iska: I do not feel that I have caused change in Doron's teaching methods; rather I have strengthened them. Doron often gives "exit ticket" tasks at the end of the lesson. When I asked him about it, he told me he had picked it up from Doug Lemov's book, *Teaching Like a Champion* (Lemov, 2010), where it serves to check pupils' understanding of the material taught in class. At Kaye College an additional benefit is that this technique helps keep the students focused, and in the classroom, to the end of the lesson. I appreciated his answer. Before the project, I never really asked why lecturers give quizzes, and now I saw the rationale.

I have implemented some of Doron's teaching methods in my practice teaching class. I saw that in his lessons, when a student does not know the answer to a question, he asks another student the same question, and after receiving a correct reply returns to the previous student and checks whether she now knows the answer. I did this in my practice teaching, and it made the pupils listen to me carefully and raised the level of attentiveness during the lesson (this is another of Lemov's suggestions). Doron also employs a lot of humor in his lessons, brings many examples from various fields, and makes methodological "breaks" for meta-teaching, to point out his own practices, why he uses them, and how they can be adapted for use in school. All these raise the class's attention and alertness.

I particularly liked the last lessons of the semester. Doron asked the students to pick two stories for study that are part of the literature component in high school. Doron encouraged the students to consider how they would teach them in school—how they would prepare, what they would emphasize, etc. These lessons had practical value. As a student I felt I could teach the stories without fear, because Doron gave ideas about what to do with the stories, which iInternet sites to use, how to explain the setting without letting the author's biography guide the teaching, how to observe enriching details such as the relation between the title and the story.

The relationship that I developed with Doron over the course of the project was important for me. I felt he was interested in my opinions, and that I could confer with him on college matters and also about personal issues. This relationship would not have existed without the willingness of Kaye College to establish a partnership project between students and lecturers. Doron also added to my sense of my own capabilities. He commended me on my awareness and sensitivity at our meetings, praised me to others (in a letter to Dr. Mansur Shahor, at a symposium at the College, etc.), and raised the level of my self-confidence. I was in tune with Doron's teaching methods, as well as his qualities. As a future teacher, I would like to implement his teaching methods, especially after having seen their advantages. Teaching is a constantly developing and flexible profession, and Doron's participation, even after years of lecturing in an academic setting, underscored the importance of the profession and that as a teacher I should not take things for granted but rather be open to changes and innovations such as this project.

SOME CONCLUSIONS

Iska: Participating in the project was rewarding beyond my expectations. I was quick to join the pilot, because I liked the idea in general, but I didn't really know what to expect and what I was supposed to do. As soon as the semester started and I met Doron, Dr. Ruthy, and the other students, I stopped worrying. During the project, I was exposed to various teaching methods and received tools that I will use as a teacher. I survived a course not in my native language, enriched my knowledge, and even used things I learned in this course in other literature courses I study.

I was also exposed to new teaching methods in Doron's lessons that I anticipate implementing in my own lessons. I started looking differently at the lessons of my other teachers. The most significant tool I received from the project is critical thinking. I have stopped taking my teachers' methods for granted and started asking myself, and occasionally them, why they chose a particular method, did it fulfill what they set out to achieve, and if they were to teach the lesson again, what would they keep and what would they change? Before the project I would sit in class like a good student, summarize the lecturer's words, and do the assignments as required. I never thought why the lecturer gave this specific assignment, or why now, and what aims it fulfills. Sitting in class now, I see things from a lecturer's or teacher's point of view as well, and think about the practice of teaching, in addition to my experience as a learner.

Last but not least, I embarked on new relationships, a close friendship with the other five students who participated in the pilot, and a warm mutual regard with Doron and Dr. Ruthy. I am truly fortunate.

Doron: Despite my initial misgivings, the student-faculty pedagogical partnership followed Horace's dictum to be both enjoyable and instructive, and to do so for both partners. That it was so, depended to no small extent on the individual partners and on the vibe between them. I too feel fortunate to have been assigned a partner with whom I could think aloud about matters that are rarely aired even among colleagues, let alone in the presence of students. While I can imagine more formal arrangements, this one was most suitable for my purposes, and I applaud the College for choosing to adopt the program. Clearly, management support for the initiative is crucial for its success (Takayama, Kaplan & Cook-Sather 2017), and in Kaye College it is slated to continue. Faculty to whom I talked about the program were curious and wanted to participate as well, so I hope it will become a regular feature of student-faculty cooperation.

My purpose from the start included achieving a glimpse of my teaching persona through another's eyes, like that elusive reflection of oneself before you know it's you—more out of an anxious curiosity than from any urgent need to reinvent myself as a teacher. But adjacent to that curiosity is also the desire for external validation, and this comes at the cost of exposure to another's gaze. The performative nature of teaching is obvious to anyone who has stood in front of a class. The difficulty is to disentwine the performative from the more substantive issues of teaching and learning. "Managing" a classroom full of students is only the prerequisite to teaching it. The true challenges emerge when the teachers question and perhaps change their deeply held beliefs and habitual behaviors. This process can occur in many ways, including in a pedagogical partnership.

Rereading our interleaved responses, it strikes me how differently we envisioned our process from the outset, how distinct our expectations, experiences, and responses were as well. Thus the dialogue between us in this chapter only gestures towards our long talks but does not fully reflect them in either form or content. Yet the critical momentum set up by the partnership has led both of us to return to the starting point of the process and to learn from it, not as repetition merely, but as a creative and learned re-vision. This re-vision is based on reflection and leads to change—to the voicing of needs, the discussion of alternatives, trial and error, and occasionally to some solutions. It is a never-ending process—all the more reason it should always be celebrated.

REFERENCES

Assaf, L., Garza, R., & Battle, J. (2010). Multicultural teacher education: Examining the perceptions, practices, and coherence in one teacher preparation program. *Teacher Education Quarterly, 37*(2), 115–135.

Camangian, P. (2010). Starting with self: Teaching autoethnography to foster critically caring literacies. *Research in the Teaching of English, 45*(2).

Cook-Sather, A. (2019). Wrestling with the languages and practices of pedagogical partnership. *Teaching and Learning Together in Higher Education, 27.*

Cook-Sather, A. & Felten, P. (2017). Where student engagement meets faculty development: How student-faculty pedagogical partnership fosters a sense of belonging. *Student Engagement in Higher Education Journal, 1*(2), 3–11.

Fukada, Y., Fukada, T., Falout, J., & Murphey, T. (2017). Collaboratively visualizing possible others. *Learner Development Journal, 1*(1), 78–93.

Howard, T. C. (2003). Relevant pedagogy: Ingredients for critical teacher reflection. *Theory into Practice, 42*(3), 195–202.

Joldersma, C., & Perhamus, L. M. (2020). Stealing an education: On the precariousness of justice. *Teachers College Record, 122*(2).

Lemov, D. (2010). *Teach like a champion: 49 techniques that put students on the path to college.* Hoboken, NJ: Wiley.

Mahboob, A. (2010). *The NNEST lens: Non-native English speakers in TESOL.* Cambridge: Cambridge University Press.

Medgyes, P. (1992). Native or non-native: Who's worth more? *ELT Journal, 46*(4), 340–349.

Moussu, L., & Llurda, E. (2008). Non-native English-speaking English language teachers: History and research. *Language and Teaching, 41*(3), 315–348.

Shulman, L S. (1986). Those who understand: Knowledge growth in teaching. *Educational Researcher, 15*(2), 4–14.

Simon, A., & Boyer, E. G. (Eds.) (1967). *Mirrors for behavior, an anthology of classroom observation instruments.* Wynote, PA: Communication Materials Center.

Stanciu, C., & Lin, A. (2017). Guest editors' introduction: Multi-ethnic literatures of the United States: Pedagogy in anxious times. *Melus, 42*(4), 1–19.

Takayama, K., Kaplan, M., & Cook-Sather, A. (2017). Advancing diversity and inclusion through strategic multilevel leadership. *Liberal Education,* 103 (3/4). http://www.aacu.org/liberaleducation/2017/summer-fall/takayama_kaplan_cook-sather.

Templeton, L., MacCracken, A., & Smith, A. (2019). A study of student voice in higher education. *Liberal Education,* 22(1). http://portal.criticalimpact.com/go/1/9b18c25f1e2580f8a6473c7b9fa19141/25043/f76570ac40934479/833c595de4d20d823947229f28c3afba.

Vogel, S. & García, O. (2017). Translanguaging. In G. Noblit & L. Moll (Eds.), *Oxford research encyclopedia of education.* Oxford: Oxford University Press.

Wragg, E.C. (2012). *An introduction to classroom observation.* London: Routledge.

Chapter Six

The Student-Faculty Partnership Program's Potential for Revitalizing the One-Shot Library Instruction Session

Amanda Eugair Peach and Ashley Ferrell

CONTEXT

Provided by Leslie Ortquist-Ahrens, Director, Center for Teaching and Learning.

Berea College is a small, private, 4-year liberal arts higher education institution, located in Berea, Kentucky, in the Appalachian region of the United States. One of the eight federally funded Work Colleges, Berea combines a 10-15 hour weekly work experience with a traditional academic education for its 1,660 students. The first interracial and coeducational college in the South, Berea College remains radical today by providing full-tuition scholarships to all accepted students, primarily from Appalachia, on the condition that they must demonstrate great academic promise but have limited economic resources.

Supported by a generous grant from the Andrew W. Mellon Foundation, and as of fall 2019, supported by an endowment, the Student-Faculty Partnerships Program is part of the work of the Center for Teaching and Learning. Since 2017, it has invited faculty, staff, and students to participate in semester-long pedagogical partnerships. Faculty or staff members agree to open one class (or, in cases where participants don't teach, a similar context) weekly for the student partner to observe; to meet one hour a week with the student partner to discuss observations and insights; and attend monthly meetings with the program co-facilitators and other faculty/staff participants to discuss their experiences. Students take the equivalent of a one-credit course with the program co-facilitators, one of whom is a faculty member at the college. In the course, they learn about teaching and learning in higher education, explore and practice listening well and giving constructive feedback, and build a small and tight community with other student partners in the program as they come to see common areas in new ways.

Since the pilot launch in the spring of 2017, 27 faculty and staff and 29 students have participated in the program in 35 partnerships (some have participated more than once). While the vast majority of partnerships have involved classroom faculty, the program has been open to administrative staff with teaching or similar assignments. The partnership, discussed in this chapter, between Amanda Peach, a librarian with faculty status, and student partner Ashley Ferrell, took place in spring 2018. Together, this was our first experience with a partnership focused less on the classroom teaching of a course, and in this case, on one-shot library instruction sessions. Since paving the way, Amanda has participated a second time with a different partner, and two additional colleagues—who are not strictly classroom faculty members—have participated in the program.

CHOICE AND FOCUS IN PARTNERSHIP

Amanda: Insecurities about my teaching ability prompted me to apply to participate in the Student-Faculty Partnership Program. At the time that I applied, I was also in the process of applying for promotion from Assistant to Associate Professor. I had spent considerable time reflecting on my past work in preparation for writing my promotion narrative, and as I did, I kept circling back to my fears that I was not leading my classroom effectively. I am an Instruction Librarian, and while bibliographic instruction is only a portion of my overall job duties, it is an essential part. My final wish in my promotion narrative, when I looked forward and named my goals for the next five or ten years, was simply stated: to become a better teacher.

My hope was to make my standardized one-shot library instruction session more engaging. Each section of the first-year research writing course, known as GSTR 210, is required to share one class session with a librarian. These sessions are only an hour long and have the impossible burden of being the place where we teach students everything they need to know about research and information literacy, along with introducing them to our library-specific resources. As such, they are information dense and fast paced, which does not allow much space for active learning. I had tried to make the sessions as interesting as possible and had been told I was doing well by both my supervisors and peers who observed me in the classroom, as well as the faculty for whom I was teaching, but I knew better. I had observed students falling asleep or missing questions on the exit assessment that they should have been able to answer after the intervention of my instruction. I knew that I was in need of real feedback—the kind that could spur a small revolution in my classroom.

Ashley: I had never heard of the Student-Faculty Partnerships Program (SFPP) before, but it sounded like it would help me focus on my own pedagogical skills. I am currently studying to become an elementary school teacher. I saw SFPP as a unique experience that would allow me to work on seeing the classroom from both experiences, as an educator and learner. SFPP also uniquely bridges relationships between students and professors. I wanted to get a more in-depth look at the inner workings of a classroom and experience a lesson from start to finish.

The focus of our partnership was on Amanda's one-shot lesson. The main goals that we set during our first meeting were to increase student engagement in the lesson, improve the assessment scores, and have a fresh set of eyes—mine—look over the lesson. My personal goal was to learn new ways to look at my own teaching, as a prospective elementary school teacher, and improve it. I wanted to become more aware of student engagement levels in a classroom.

I chose to work in this partnership because Amanda convinced me. She told me how good I would be at it and that we could create something new together. I am a little self-conscious about trying new things or putting myself in a position to do something I am not sure I can do well. Having Amanda's encouragement early on set the tone for our partnership. I was a little hesitant to start because I was afraid I was not going to have enough time to accommodate both of our schedules. Amanda's classes were unpredictable and did not meet at the same time every week. They were scheduled based on the needs of the teaching faculty who brought their classes to the library, at their convenience. That meant that each and every week I had to look at that week's schedule and then pick the one that fit my schedule the best. It took strategic planning on both of our parts in order to find which session would fit best each week.

UNFOLDING THE PARTNERSHIP

Amanda: Up until the SFPP, peer and faculty evaluations of me as a classroom teacher had been kind but unhelpful. Examples of such feedback were comments like "great choices of databases," "funny," and "enthusiastic." My peers were simply too easy on me, maybe because they empathized with me, having themselves struggled with cramming a semester's worth of content into one class session? Or perhaps they feared the repercussions of giving negative feedback to a peer they work with every day? Or, just maybe, they didn't recognize those moments when I was relying on jargon or assuming prior knowledge of our students because they have that same knowledge and so they are unconscious of it? I knew I needed an outsider to observe me, someone removed from all of those concerns.

I asked Ashley to be my partner, rather than wait to be randomly assigned one by the program. At the time, Ashley was the Student Supervisor for the Technology Help Desk and Reference Desk at Hutchins Library. As her direct supervisor, I had shared the floor with her at our department training meetings and had been impressed by the way she organized lessons and articulated learning objectives each time she taught her peers. As I observed her teach, it was clear to me that as an upper-level education major, she had already spent more time actively contemplating pedagogy than I had. It had been more than a decade since I had completed my one required Instructional Methods course as a part of my Library Science degree curriculum; choosing Ashley as my partner provided an inroad into current scholarship in the field of education.

When Ashley and I first met, my goal was vague in nature. I told Ashley that I wanted to be a better teacher. Ashley talked me through the process of defining that so that we could arrive at a goal that was actionable and measurable. I decided that I wanted to create a more student-centered classroom, but I was sure that too little time coupled with too much content were barriers to my achieving this. In response, Ashley promised to observe how I spent my time in class to see if we could discover places that would lend themselves to being streamlined in order to free up time for active learning exercises.

Ashley: Amanda and I unknowingly started earlier than the rest of our cohort. We were both so excited and eager that we just jumped into the program and started evaluating her lessons immediately. The first week I was in her classroom, Amanda asked me to start by just looking at timing and pacing in her lesson. She mentioned that she had always wanted to do a jigsaw exercise but did not know how to go about it. She did not think there was enough time for it. After observing several sessions of hers, I compared my notes from each and found a pattern. She spent a lot of time addressing questions that would appear at the end of the lesson in the exit assessment, especially question one, which was the most frequently missed question on both the pre- and post-assessments.

The question asked which of several options was the most effective method for locating full-text, peer-reviewed articles on the topic of DNA structure, and it was not addressed succinctly; it took her 17 total minutes to address each of the potential answers and those minutes were spread out across the entire 50-minute session. Students did not realize that the answers were interconnected because of the drawn-out way they were addressed. We decided this was an ideal place to change her approach, and so we took each of the possible answers for the question and turned it into a jigsaw. We split the classroom into small groups or dyads, with each group assigned just one of the possible answers to try. After three minutes, the groups were invited to share their findings with the entire class. As the groups demonstrated how to use a particular method (for example, using Google) to their peers, they also addressed the effectiveness of the method they had been assigned. After each of the options had been presented, students weighed in on which had been most successful. They were talking and engaged, time was shaved off the presentation of the material (even with each group presenting, the average time saved was three minutes per class), and student performance on the exit assessment improved.

Exit slips were another big change to Amanda's lesson plan. I thought they would prove invaluable because I believe the best way to find out what students don't know is to ask them. However, Amanda was afraid they were futile. Her concern was that the nature of the one-shot meant that even if students raised good questions or made useful suggestions on the exit slip, they would never hear the answer to their question or see their recommendations implemented. Plus, when she had used exit slips intermittently in the past, it felt like students always asked the same questions, such as "How do I cite?" This was frustrating to her since she always made a point of saying at some point during the lesson that she does not teach citations. She wasn't sold on the usefulness of these slips if there was nothing new to glean from them.

After we talked it through, though, we decided on a solution. If, when reviewing the exit slips after class, she found that students had asked questions that needed answers, then Amanda could email their professor, providing them the answer and asking them to relay it to their entire class, so all could potentially benefit. Also, instead of being bothered by students asking about citations, we decided Amanda could add a small blurb to her presentation about where students could go if they needed further help with citations—specifically, to the Writing Center, which is also located in the library. Once that content was added to the lesson, the number of future students who asked that question on the exit slip dwindled. With that need satisfied, students were able to stop asking about citations and move on to deeper questions that required contemplation, such as, "How do you recommend I read wordy academic journals more efficiently?"

INSIGHTS GAINED ABOUT WORKING IN PARTNERSHIP

Amanda: I was surprised by how emotionally taxing the experience of collaboration was. I had enough self-awareness to know that I might struggle with receiving constructive criticism, but what I did not anticipate was how much my student partner's opinion about me would come to mean to me. She always handled the process of post-instruction feedback with professionalism and respect, but I still managed to cry a few times when we discussed the dissonance between my plans for a class session and the ways I actually executed them. It mattered to me greatly that my partner should know how much I cared about my work, how much I longed to improve, and how seriously I would take her suggestions.

Ashley: We were lucky that we already had a relationship going into this program. In order for the partnership to be successful, you have to have a level of trust. Even though we worked together before this program, I was still nervous about giving feedback. I knew that I wanted it to be appropriate, but I never wanted it to come from a place of ill-intent. I never wanted it to come across as I know better than the person who is teaching in this class-room. That was one of my challenges in the beginning because I wanted to give good feedback that helped the partnership move forward, but I always wanted to be conscious that I was not overstepping any boundaries or having my feedback come across in a way I did not intend.

I learned just how much work goes into making partnerships and collabo-rations run smoothly. Throughout this partnership, we would make one small change, thinking it was going to make a big difference and everything would be great from here on out. But, once one issue was 'fixed,' it cleared up the way for something else to be identified. Every week, it felt like there was something new that needed to be investigated, explored, and considered in order to accomplish the outcome that Amanda envisioned. Also, it was not until about a month after our partnership ended that Amanda came to me and said that her lesson finally looked the way she wanted it to.

INSIGHTS GAINED INTO LEARNING AND TEACHING

Amanda: The partnership provided me with space I needed to question the way I had been teaching. Eight years earlier, during my first month at Berea College, our library instruction program coordinator left. We were short-staffed for a year afterward, and so my first year as an Instruction Librarian at Hutchins Library was all about survival. I had inherited a script and Power-Point from my predecessor, and I just got up in front of one class after another, delivering this content I had not created. Over the years, I tweaked it, adding to it, but never cutting anything or challenging existing content because by then, our teaching faculty had come to rely on the librarians to deliver that specific information. I feared resistance from both the teaching faculty who shared their classes with me, as well as the other instruction librarians if I changed the curriculum too dramatically. With participation in the SFPP, however, I suddenly had an excuse to consider substantive changes; I could say that the program required this reflection on my part.

One of the first significant changes I implemented was removing content from my lesson. It felt counterintuitive to teach even less material when my limited time frame meant that I was already sacrificing content that I considered indispensable. As Ashley observed and reported back to me about the periods in which students were the least engaged, however, it became clear to me that teaching them a whole lot, which they weren't absorbing or connecting with, was ineffective. Information literacy skills can help students be more critical consumers and users of information, which is invaluable throughout their school careers and after. Those skills cannot be developed, though, when students cannot hear the message. For that reason, I abandoned a part of my vision of the ideal research process. The Hutchins librarians have long argued that research should begin with perusing entries in specialized encyclopedias to gain base knowledge on a topic before then chasing down sources cited in the bibliographies of those entries. I believed it, so I spent a significant portion of the one-shot demonstrating this technique. Ashley, though, noticing how much time was given to this method, questioned that investment. She questioned the relevance of this part of the lesson when most faculty outright forbade students from citing reference books.

Ashley: It was after my first observation that I asked Amanda if she would ever consider removing the encyclopedias from her one-shot. The librarians' reasons for teaching them as a part of the research process were logical, but from my perspective as a student, I had concerns informed by an understanding of what professors are actually asking for in the papers that they assign. They almost exclusively require students to use peer-reviewed scholarly articles, not tertiary reference books. As a senior, I had only ever had one professor who allowed us to use reference materials, and I knew I was not alone. I was able to report back to Amanda that students were unengaged when she lectured about encyclopedias and wondered if that lack of interest was due to a lack of applicability for them. If she were to cut this content out of her lesson, it might free up time for the jigsaw exercise, which could focus on teaching students how to find the sources they were actually required to use.

As a student, I was able to see all the background work that goes into making a lesson. I saw how often instructors have to revisit the same idea or exercise until it finally works the way it is envisioned. Also, in Amanda's case, I witnessed the difficulty of planning a lesson for students she did not know while trying to meet their needs. I saw how uncomfortable it can be to change. It is easy to get into a routine of how your lesson should go and any sort of change throws everything off. Change can make someone self-conscious about their abilities. I saw how much work goes into preparing lessons and how much we had to change. It made me more understanding of other professors.

Through this partnership, my views on student learning were affirmed. I was able to witness firsthand why student-centered lessons were important and the benefits they bring to students. Through Amanda, I was able to experiment with some of my pedagogical beliefs and see them play out in a college class instead of an elementary classroom, where I normally observe. We were able to affirm that students learn better through guided exercises where they teach themselves and their peers with support. This was proven through the improved assessment scores and through the sounds of animated discussion between students during the jigsaw exercise.

ADVICE ABOUT PARTNERSHIPS

Amanda

Challenges

Beyond the vulnerability of being scrutinized by my student partner while teaching, I also struggled with insecurity regarding the reception I believed I would receive from faculty peers in the program. The faculty cohort participating in our program only met away from our student partners a handful of times throughout the semester, but I dreaded our first meeting. Some teaching faculty do not consider librarians to be their academic equals, and so I worried about admitting to these "real" teaching faculty that I doubted my effectiveness as an instructor. I worried that doing so might reinforce any existing notions they might have about my illegitimacy as a teacher. Related to that, I feared faculty might second-guess sharing their class sessions with me in the future as a result.

If faculty did actually think those things, they never said so. It was a welcome, but humbling, realization when I understood that no one was as concerned with my imposter status as I was. With each passing class observation and subsequent feedback planning session with Ashley, I grew more invested in the change that we were cultivating. Implementing, reflecting on, and then tweaking the lesson every week was such a time investment that I just no longer had time to worry about those initial fears.

I would advise anyone participating in a partnership to be transparent about the process with their colleagues and their students. I tried to give faculty advance notice, when possible, that my student partner would be sitting in on their class session with me. When they arrived with their students for a bibliographic session, I always began by introducing myself and then Ashley, who would be sitting in the back of the room. I told them Ashley was observing my teaching because I had a goal of making these sessions more engaging. Further, I warned them that even if they had attended sessions like this before, it might be different than they expected because we were implementing new ideas. Faculty know how difficult it can be to implement change and students know how historically dull these sessions could be, so I thought both would appreciate and benefit from knowing why I was making certain choices. Giving them advance notice relieved me from worrying about how they were interpreting my lesson from minute-to-minute.

Benefits

Each time I pursue a professional development opportunity, my hope is to have one small takeaway that helps me perform some aspect of my work better. The changes Ashley and I implemented surpassed those modest hopes. We made several changes, big and small, the sum of which was the real gain: a sense of ownership over this new iteration of the one-shot lesson plan. This, in turn, fostered a renewed passion for work which had grown to feel rote and like an obligation more than anything. To feel a new and deeper connection to my work was a gift; the partnership process that got me there taught me that I am capable of growth and change, as well as confronting my fear.

   I would advise faculty engaging in partnership to take their student partner's suggestions to heart, even if they contradict your experience or instincts. If you are brave enough to participate in the partnership, then you must be longing for some real and substantive change and that change is not as likely to occur if you stick with what feels comfortable. Nothing is permanent or unfixable, so why not chance it and approach your teaching or a lesson based on your student's perspective? For example, I had almost a decade of experience informing my decision to not use exit slips in one-shot instruction sessions, but Ashley asked me to try again and I reluctantly agreed. Ashley challenged me to use the information gleaned from those slips differently than I had in the past and when I did, it made a powerful difference. She was right! Instead of focusing on what didn't work with the slips (the fact that I would never see that exact class again and thus could not share answers with them), she showed me how I could incorporate the answer to common exit slip questions in my future lessons, so at least future students wouldn't have to leave a session with those questions unanswered. It seems so obvious, but I had missed it. Now that I have incorporated that change for more than a year, it feels like second nature to me, like I have always taught that way. The students are better off for it and I owe that change in my classroom to Ashley's powerful insight.

Ashley

Challenges

I was worried at the beginning that I was going to be unable to meet my other obligations if I added the SFPP to an already full schedule. However, the program only took three hours a week, which is less time than I would have spent in other classes. Furthermore, because my faculty partner and I worked on accommodating each other's time and needs, we worked well together.

The biggest challenge, in the beginning, was meeting the feedback needs of my partner. I wanted to give feedback that was constructive and positive. I eventually figured out the best way to give feedback was by asking questions about what I saw. This made sense to me because I wanted to learn more about her teaching style. When I asked her why she did something, we were both able to fully think through the importance and then move on to find a different way if needed.

Benefits

So many amazing things have come from my involvement in this program. I had the opportunity to write and publish an article with Amanda. We then presented at a conference and hopefully convinced other librarians to follow in our footsteps. At Berea, there were two other librarian/student partnerships that came from our involvement. The most recent opportunity that has come from being involved in this program is the opportunity to write this piece. It has always been a goal of mine to write and present but I did not know how to get started. SFPP has given me the opportunity to complete my professional goals. Also, it has been amazing to share my experiences with other librarians and my peers. I want them to know about the amazing growth that can happen from being a part of this program. I learned a lot about myself and about my pedagogy. With each new phase of this program; the actual partnership, the presentation, the article, and now this chapter, I have learned something new about this program and the benefits it has given me. Also, I have gained a deeper understanding of pedagogy, teaching, and learning. I have established what I believe about pedagogy, and I have instances from this program to support that belief. I have seen teaching and learning from both sides, and I am able to step back in my own teaching and think about what a student would say if they were giving me feedback like I gave Amanda in this program. I have seen the benefits of student-centered instruction and from stepping back to take a look at teaching. I have also seen the benefits of asking someone to intensely critique your work in the classroom and when given explicit goals that they can be reached.

As a student, this program was invaluable. Not only did it serve as a great item on my resume and a unique talking point for interviews, but it strengthened my connection to my school community. I was able to work with other student mentors within my cohort who were from outside of my discipline, which meant their feedback came from a different perspective that I had not considered before. As an education major, I am surrounded by people who think the same way as me about how to look at classroom management styles. This program allowed me to experience how other disciplines see the classroom. My advice to students wanting to do this is to jump in. There is so much you can learn about yourself, teaching, and learning through SFPP.

Chapter Seven

Untangling the Power Dynamics in Forging Student-Faculty Collaboration

Amrita Kaur and Toh Yong Bing

CONTEXT

This chapter offers reflections on a student-faculty collaboration that unfolded at a large public university in the northern state of Malaysia. The university has 16 comprehensive faculties offering undergraduate and postgraduate programs across disciplines in the social sciences. The university's teaching and learning centers resolutely promote Scholarship of Teaching and Learning (SoTL) across various disciplines; however, student-faculty collaboration for teaching and learning is still in its infancy. So far, six collaborations across three programs in the university have been established. This chapter focuses on the fourth collaboration in the Educational Psychology Department in which the faculty author has participated, which lasted for two semesters.

INTRODUCTION

The partnership about which we write was carried out at the course level and involved one faculty member (Amrita) and one student (Toh). While this is Amrita's fourth collaboration in the same department, it is Toh's first such experience. Amrita teaches postgraduate courses in educational psychology and is a visiting scholar, and Toh is enrolled as a master's student in the educational psychology program. In this chapter we share our collective effort in building a partnership to revise and improve the classroom instructional practices and discuss how the revisions were beneficial for both of us.

FOCUS AND GOAL OF THE PARTNERSHIP WORK

Amrita: As noted above, this was my fourth partnership with students, and I have noticed that these partnerships did not only benefit students through fostering enhanced motivation, engagement, and learning but also enriched my teaching experiences. Through these collaborations I am able to engage my students intrinsically and together we seek ways to create meaningful learning experiences. Therefore, given that valuable experience, I am always keen on building such collaborations. Additionally, I am a visiting scholar (foreigner) to Universiti Utara Malaysia, and being a foreigner, I am always interested in understanding teaching and learning from students' native cultural point of view.

Toh is pursuing his master's degree by research, and I have known him since he attended mandatory courses in educational psychology with me in February 2018. In October 2018 he approached me with a request to voluntarily sit in on additional classes to gain more subject-matter knowledge. Knowing Toh as a student with a profound interest in learning, I immediately accepted his request and invited him to participate as my instructional consultant. The fact that Toh was not to be graded for this course assured me that he would be candid and honest in providing feedback. However, given the current cultural context where a teacher is always right, it took me some time to persuade Toh to embrace the new role. I urged him to read the literature on partnerships and think about the benefits of participating in such collaborations. Later, I met him face to face to try to better understand his reservations so that we, in our traditional context, could function as effectively as the Western counterparts did in their partnerships. I also assured him that we could participate in partnership without harming our traditional positions.

This instructional design collaboration required Toh to act as a pedagogical consultant by actively participating in the class activities and later providing feedback on the activities' effectiveness. I have always felt that the end-of-the-course evaluations do not serve the purpose of enhancing teaching and learning practices well for several reasons. One, they measure general questions in quantitative ways, and two, since they are conducted at the end of the course they do not offer any opportunity to make improvements. With this partnership, I was able to receive continuous, qualitative feedback—textual and descriptive reflections of my teaching practices rather than a number on scale—and I also had the opportunity to view my instruction through the eyes of a student. This combination helped me plan my next lesson in a better way.

Toh: I have always been passionate about higher education and adult learning. My master's degree in education provided me the opportunity to look more deeply into adult learning. For that reason, when Dr. Amrita invited me to provide feedback on the 'Learning and Individual Differences' course she had taught for a long time, I was both excited and hesitant about the opportunity. I was hesitant because the invitation was unusual and sounded quite radical to me, since it is not something common in our culture. Despite this, I decided to take up the challenge.

The traditional concept of faculty and student's relationship is hierarchical, formal, and rigid. The faculty could be friendly but never be friends with a student. They teach, guide, facilitate, comment, correct, and are accountable for students' academic performance, but students cannot take on those roles for faculty. Even though we understand that teachers have certain limitations, Malaysian students generally view teachers or lecturers as people who have the authority and are the knowledge bearers. We are taught at a young age to show respect, listen, and obey, rather than question them. So, questioning or disagreeing with your teachers is a "no no." Our curiosity or need to question must be restrained and reframed on most occasions. Therefore, my brain automatically began to generate numerous thoughts! Why? Why me? I have no formal teaching experience; I am inexperienced, what is there that I could contribute to her teaching? Will she value my comments as constructive, or will she give me a frown?

Overall, I was intimidated and overwhelmed! However, I was convinced that my experience as a student could be helpful in speaking for the majority in our context. So, with Dr. Amrita's persuasion, I agreed to take on this new role. Dr. Amrita provided me a list of reflection pointers such as to indicate appropriateness and effectiveness of teaching curriculum, content, activities, assessments, classroom environment, interaction, and above all what could have been done in a better way.

BUILDING OUR PARTNERSHIP

Amrita: In getting started with our partnership, my first meeting with Toh was focused on clarifying our roles, building reciprocity, and clarifying expected outcomes of the collaboration. Introduction of such threshold concepts in education, in Asian settings, requires careful consideration of words to explain the process. I assured Toh that his feedback would be valuable, beneficial for everyone in the class, and would not offend me in any way. I also shared literature on student-faculty partnerships with him to help him envisage its possible implementation in our context. For effective implementation of this partnership, we also looked into some of the Western models of students as pedagogical consultants whereby students sit away from the rest of the students, probably at the back of the classroom, and take observation notes. Toh revealed that taking on this role as a student required courage due to his cultural disposition, which he felt he didn't have then. But, finally, Toh agreed to sit through the classes. However, he chose to participate in all the activities and assignments with other students in the class and did not reveal his role of consultant to other students in the class.

This anonymity helped Toh in two ways. One, he was saved from cultural awkwardness of 'a student observing a teacher's teaching.' Two, he was able to elicit other students' feedback and get into dialogue regarding classroom instruction and students' experiences. Toh kept a regular journal of his observational feedback based on the prompts we both had agreed on. He usually reflected on those prompts soon after the class ended. The prompts included questions like: What was the most effective activity? Was the assessment appropriate? What was classroom interaction like? What are things that could have been done better and how? His major observations were focused on classroom instruction, assessment practices, and my interaction with other students. The semester was 12 weeks long, and during this period we constantly remained in touch via email and WhatsApp. We had three face-to-face meetings where Toh shared his feedback on my instruction on which I took notes, and I also audio recorded his responses with his permission. After a few sessions, I could feel Toh settling into his new role and our conversation became more comfortable and less formal.

Toh: I had experienced Dr. Amrita's classes earlier, and I was inspired by the enthusiasm and passion she demonstrates for teaching; thus, I thought the offer to serve as an instructional consultant was worth considering. The day before our first face-to-face, feedback-sharing meeting, I devoted much time to listing my observations and reflections on the classes I had attended. I carefully rehearsed in my mind how to articulate my suggestions correctly and respectfully. Though the discussion was a casual and informal sharing session, I reluctantly but sensitively voiced my opinions. I slowly went through my list of points one by one, and I skipped some that I felt were a bit too critical. I constructed my words carefully and tried to avoid saying anything meaningless or offensive. As we continued our discussion, I sensed Dr. Amrita's openness through attentive and positive responses. Because of the way she responded, I became more willing and courageous to share that more critical feedback that I had left out earlier. Eventually, through this process, I gained confidence. Dr. Amrita's willingness to hear let me speak my mind effortlessly and meaningfully.

INSIGHTS ABOUT WORKING IN PARTNERSHIP

Amrita: Working in partnership, especially in the current one, has made me realize that faculty in higher education, with their students who are adults, mature, and with a variety of experiences, have an immense advantage of incorporating their ideas to design and innovate contextually meaningful pedagogical practices. In my case, I may be the pedagogical expert, but my students, who are in-service or pre-service teachers with a clear understanding of human learning principles, have an amazing potential to contribute to collaboration for effective instruction.

These partnerships are ideal for increasing student-faculty interaction and nurturing belongingness, which are highly recommended as among the components of high-impact teaching practices. I felt that by the end of this partnership with Toh, our interactions, instead of being deliberate like in the beginning, had evolved into more spontaneous, mutually stimulating, and fulfilling experiences. I also noticed that the elements of trust and accountability, which are fundamental in adult education, can be fostered efficiently through such collaborations. During this collaborative process, Toh and I achieved a balance between traditional power and contemporary agency to function responsibly in each of our roles. Instead of interpreting Toh's suggestions as criticism, I showed trust in his ability to provide suggestions and incorporated them into my practice with positive results.

Additionally, such partnerships can be immensely valuable for foreign scholars like me who are not native to university or national culture. Engaging local students can provide insights for culturally responsive pedagogy. Having Toh as a pedagogical consultant, who was also an active student in the class, worked as an inspirational agent for other students to be actively engaged. His role helped me forge closer connections with other students. All in all, the outcomes are reciprocal and benefit both the parties.

Toh: The traditional and cultural understanding of teachers being the knowledge-bearers who have greater authority and should be respected as well as obeyed still has a tight grasp on me. As a result, in the beginning, this concept of partnership between teacher and student was unthinkable for me. Given the hierarchy and power in my context, it is often hard to undertake a casual discussion on things at the same level. Thus, the idea of sharing opinions, providing feedback on what was good or what needed to be changed, was a tough one. On top of that, I was skeptical about my expertise such as how I could contribute to the practice of someone who has taught the course a long time.

Fortunately, I was able to overcome my skepticism and revise my assumptions. For instance, I had certain questions as well as suggestions regarding an activity Dr. Amrita always does in the beginning of her class. I had a feeling that this activity could be made more meaningful. Then I stepped back, thinking that she might have good reasons for doing it her way. However, after further thought, I decided to go ahead and discuss my thoughts with her. The next morning, when we met up in her office, to my surprise she was extremely impressed with my proposal and acknowledged its value. This experience reinforced my belief in myself and my ability to think critically. Her positive comments and response boosted my confidence. In addition to this experience, Dr. Amrita's attentiveness and appreciative responses as I shared my opinions throughout this partnership convinced me that I am capable of contributing my opinions. Moreover, when she incorporated my suggestions in her subsequent lessons, I became more convinced that my contributions were valuable, and my efforts were meaningful.

Another important factor that reinforced my intention to continue was that this partnership was not merely a mandatory academic exercise for Dr. Amrita. Instead, it was her personal endeavor to improve her teaching and learning. It reassured me about her sincerity in this undertaking and inviting me to be a part of it.

My partnership with Dr. Amrita also improved my experience and practice as a student. It has provided me an opportunity to assume a more proactive and critical role in reflecting on what I have learned and hence made me more accountable and conscious of my learning. I believe that it has enhanced my metacognition and self-regulation for my learning. I can now think more clearly about the learning process, and I can plan it more effectively. The partnership has taught me to view myself differently. The active process of viewing teaching and learning through a critical lens greatly influenced the way I view my relationship with the course, the teacher, and the students.

For these reasons, this partnership was beneficial to both of us. While I have gained numerous insights into the content as well as the learning process and have grown personally, my faculty partner has equally benefited. If all lecturers could view students' responses and feedback as their teaching resources, they would learn from their students' input. Those responses can be helpful in improving faculty's teaching approaches, quality, and application of the teaching content. I believe, in Asian culture, it is the teachers' prerogative to bring this paradigm shift, i.e., to start believing that students are not merely the passive receivers of knowledge, but are contributors and valuable resources for teaching. Additionally, by seeking students' critical opinions with a different perspective, not as something threatening to their authority, they can celebrate that as an opportunity to understand students' needs. Meanwhile, students who wish to participate in such a partnership have to start believing in themselves and critically challenge their own concept of learning and its construction.   .

INSIGHTS INTO LEARNING AND TEACHING

Amrita: Throughout the partnership, the reciprocal feedback mechanism Toh and I developed shaped my classroom instruction and students' learning experiences in a meaningful way. We ensured that we discussed Toh's observations, either online or face to face, after each session. Toh took the lead in explaining his observations and making suggestions for improvements. Later, we both deliberated on the ways to best incorporate those suggestions into the next class. We also collaboratively discussed the effectiveness—the successes as well as the weaknesses—once those propositions were tried in the class.

I was so glad that Toh's feedback provided me a window into students' hearts and minds. There were a few things that he brought to my attention that I might have ignored otherwise. For example, Toh highlighted the need for observing a short silence in between my lectures to give students a chance to reflect and make meaning about what has been said. As a result of this feedback, I divided key concepts to be taught into small segments with short pauses in between. This provided students with opportunities to reflect upon the newly learnt concepts before moving on to the next. I had always assumed that students appreciate more information and they can follow my pace in receiving information and processing it to make meaning, but this partnership made me question and reconsider some of my instructional practices.

The partnership also provided me the courage to step into a new zone where teaching and learning were a collective enterprise, and I could enrich them with the perspectives of students who have different backgrounds. For example, the course we worked on together was about learning and individual differences. The content discussion in it is usually limited to cognitive and affective domains in psychology. Toh, being from a minority community in Malaysia, was able to draw my attention to the importance of highlighting the social differences in Malaysian society and ways to handle those differences through educational initiatives. Malaysia is a multi-racial society, which comprises three major ethnic groups—Malays, Chinese, and Indians. The three of them share different cultural and religious values; however, they often seek ways to enhance social cohesion. Toh recommended that I use this course as a platform to appreciate those differences.

There were several other areas, such as my assessment and feedback practices, on which I gained valuable insights from our dialogue. For instance, we exchanged views on why a certain way of assessment was important from my perspective while students' perspective was different. I had always believed that short quizzes promote memorization and surface learning approaches until Toh explained to me its value for students in terms of learning and mastery and recommended that I have it often at the end of the lesson. Later, I did run my own research and understood the benefits of incorporating short quizzes in my classes. Through our dialogues, we were able to construe a new understanding of assessment, ways of constructing it, and its relevance to students.

Toh: As our communications went on, this partnership process provided me with an enhanced understanding of teaching and learning. Slowly, I began to realize the value of being in partnership with a faculty member. It is a rare opportunity for a student to be able to communicate thoughts on teaching and learning and contribute students' voices to the faculty member's thinking and practice. This method, I thought, was much superior in comparison to the formal course evaluation that is done only at the end of the semester. I observed that the feedback and dialogues during the partnership have hugely impacted the instructional practices in the course.

One exchange illustrates this impact. During one of our face-to-face sessions, I highlighted that Dr. Amrita shared too many concepts and too much content in one presentation. While that information might be meaningful and inspiring, it can be difficult for some students to absorb. Through our dialogue, we agreed to focus on a few concepts but would allow in-depth discussions. In the next few weeks, I could see that this approach helped students to think deeper and in broader ways and to make meaningful connections. The suggestions I made were incorporated right in the next class without having to delay and implement them in the following semester.

In addition to this kind of dialogue between me and Dr. Amrita, I also realized that all students are capable of contributing critical inputs to the course, since we are the end users of the course. Students from different backgrounds and unique experiences can see the course from different angles, and therefore, have the potential to enrich the course and its delivery. In addition, students can contribute to making the course more relevant and contextualized; for example, in my case, I saw how the course content could help in bridging our societal differences since Dr. Amrita is a visiting scholar (foreigner) and may not fully comprehend the national challenges as I do. Lastly, I realized that students can be viewed as a resource to draw advantages for the course and its delivery, since there are always blind spots or areas for improvements that the faculty might be unaware of during classes.

This collaborating process has made me realize how much I had been trapped by the cultural view that students know less than the instructor. That belief had greatly affected my learning. It restrained me from believing in my learning capabilities and what constitutes learning. As a result of participating in this partnership with Dr. Amrita, I have found myself taking more proactive roles in the learning of another course and making connections. I have become more courageous in sharing critical thoughts, asking challenging questions, and creating discussion forums with ease. Now that I am beyond this partnership, I question myself, trying to understand why I viewed myself as an "ignorant" student who has nothing significant to contribute to the learning process. Why couldn't I see myself as a resource who could help improve the quality of my education? And how teacher and student can switch roles to gain each other's perspectives to improve the teaching and learning process? In other words, I have come to believe that a teaching and learning paradigm shift could be achieved, and transformation can be reached through teacher-student partnership, in my cultural context as well.

ADVICE FOR OTHERS

Amrita: The concept of partnership is unconventional in many ways, especially in the educational contexts where respect for hierarchy and power distances are huge. The resistance from colleagues and students may sometimes dissuade the spirit of interested persons. For example, in convincing students to agree to participate in such partnerships, respect and hierarchy can pose a challenge, but the more complex task is to enhance students' beliefs about being able to contribute meaningfully. However, adopting a sensitive approach that helps build trust and assure students of their capabilities can motivate them to participate actively in such collaborations. Faculty's assurance to students that they are open to receiving feedback and work collaboratively can help foster meaningful partnerships.

Further, to persuade the departmental or institutional management to believe in such an initiative and having faculty relinquish or share their authority with students can be arduous. However, sharing the outcomes of such initiatives, which are enormously beneficial for academic and student development with those who are skeptical about this approach, can bring an attitudinal change. In our context, I believe that establishing a community of practices at university level to have students and faculty teams share their experiences with other interested individuals will dissipate the reservations and promote a positive culture for such partnerships. Institutional policies and initiatives across departments would provide opportunities for the wider student body to participate and engage meaningfully in students-faculty partnerships.

Toh: I have a few insights for others who wish to undertake such partnerships in the future, especially in our context. The first consideration is the lecturer's openness, humility, and desire to share her control of class and authority with students. Those are key to such initiatives. Connected to these attitudes is a willingness to change; this is another prerequisite for improvement that also opens up opportunities for transformation to take place. The humility of the lecturer, in such partnerships, signifies their sincerity and determination to improve things for the students. If students observe that the teacher is flexible, willing to change, and open to learning together, rather than bent on dictating, real partnership can be established. This was what Dr. Amrita showed me during the process, and it led to a successful partnership. The second key criterion is the lecturer's ability to help the student partners feel competent and confident in themselves, because students usually perceive themselves as inferior in terms of their skills and knowledge. Therefore, unless students are affirmed for our competence, it is challenging for us to provide feedback and share views that are different from our teachers' views.

Nevertheless, meaningful partnership is not possible without students demonstrating the courage and willingness to take a step forward. In the Asian context, such endeavors require courage, as it is a risky, unknown, and uncomfortable zone for us. Even though such invitations from lecturers are considered a privilege, there is an "invisible boundary" that sometimes students may not know how to respect. The risk of jeopardizing the relationship will always be a threat.

Finally, I anticipate student-faculty partnerships could bring transformation to Malaysian teaching and learning processes in higher education. We could transform traditional one-way and hierarchical pedagogical methods and pave ways for pedagogical methods that are co-constructed with students. With this, students will experience more autonomy and willingness to take ownership in their learning process.

Chapter Eight

Student as Co-designer

Processes of Planning and Teaching with the Student in Mind

Yasira Waqar and Abdul Moeed Asad

CONTEXT

Provided by Ayesha Shahid, Program Associate Academics, School of Education, LUMS.

Pedagogical Partnership Program is one of the initiatives under the newly formed Lahore University of Management Sciences (LUMS) Learning Institute. This program is currently being created in an effort to institutionalize the different types of student-faculty partnerships that already exist within LUMS and to provide an overall framework for facilitating such partnerships. The ethos of the program, drawing from the literature on this subject, is to support faculty in engaging students as co-learners, co-researchers, co-inquirers, co-developers, and co-designers (Healey, Flint, & Harrington, 2016). At the School of Education (SOE), this has emerged as a model for student collaboration in which faculty members work closely with students on various research activities, including grant writing, research synthesis, data collection, and analysis. The objective of this program is for students to benefit from a mentored relationship with faculty and for them to rise to the level of peers for faculty. Faculty and student partners have piloted curriculum-focused projects as well, such as the one described in this chapter.

THE NEW ROLE OF STUDENT AS CO-DESIGNER OF A COURSE

Yasira: As a teacher, I always maintain a friendly relationship with my students, and I try to reduce the hierarchy by encouraging the students to share their feedback on pedagogical approaches. However, student-faculty partnership was a completely new idea for me. As part of its new Learning Institute, the LUMS SOE was encouraging its faculty to work with students as partners, and a small stipend was paid to the students from the school for their participation. Support from the management is critical for the success of partnership (Takayama, Kaplan, & Cook-Sather 2017), and I was lucky to be one of the pioneers in this program. I had not read extensive research in this area, but what motivated me the most was the possibility of having someone with whom I could discuss course design and pedagogical approaches grounded in their real classroom experiences. One of my former students, Moeed, had recently shown interest in working on a project in the summer, and he was also going to be the teacher assistant for my course. I saw this as a good fit for us to work together in partnership to improve my course. Moeed's major is Computer Science, so he has not taken a lot of education courses, but since he had taken this course, I was positive that as a former student he would bring valuable insights.

Although I had been excited about discussing my course with a student, the first meeting with Moeed was the most difficult, as I found myself feeling uncomfortable discussing possible improvements in the course with my former student. Admitting as a professor that there are weaknesses in the course that can be strengthened made me vulnerable in front of my student. Holding a doctorate bestowed authority, and it was difficult to challenge it by seeking undergraduate student advice on course revision, but I proceeded with the partnership.

Moeed had the outline of the course already with him, and he knew the readings. We started with a brief overview of the course, and then I told him that I wanted to revise the course during the summer as I was not happy with the last offering. Moeed agreed with me and said that he also thought certain aspects of the course could be improved. Our agreement put me at ease as both of us had a common goal to incorporate activities in the course.

We exposed further areas for improvement that were addressed at later points when the semester started. Moeed's experience of the course gave him an authority that any new person would not have. It was the authority to back his ideas with his experience, as a student, and the authority of being an observer and a facilitator in the course.

Although the School of Education was encouraging this partnership work, there were no clear guidelines, so it was up to the faculty to decide the details of the partnership. This freedom led me to experiment with partnership, though I was apprehensive at times about whether I was following the right approach.

Moeed: I am a third-year undergraduate student majoring in Computer Science. Somewhat serendipitously, I took an education course as a free-elective in my sophomore fall semester when my friends mainly took math or business courses, and the field captured my imagination in a way other free-electives have not been able to. By the end of the academic year I had taken two education courses with Dr. Yasira, and I had enjoyed both. I expressed an interest in working on a project related to education in the summer. So, when the opportunity to work on student partnership came up, it seemed to be a perfect fit because I would get the chance to apply what I had learned. Since I had already taken this course, I had a clear understanding of the flow of the classroom sessions, and I had experienced what worked for me and had ideas about what improvements could be made. I was really motivated to work on course redesign because I had wanted another opportunity to engage with course content, and what could be more exciting than to get to apply pedagogical techniques in delivering course content in the same course where I had learned about pedagogical techniques? I was also going to be the TA for this course in the fall, and it seemed far more fulfilling to be involved in course design and in conducting activities as a TA than just marking attendance of students while sitting at the back of the class.

Slightly comical was that this partnership was for the course "Curriculum: Teaching and Learning," and the task was to redesign this course. The course redesign process was, therefore, going to be a deeply reflective process on both the resource material for the course and the experience of taking the course. After every lesson, there would be an opportunity for the faculty and student partner to look back and see if the theories of the course were being put into practice. Reflection then became a process, and it eventually became part of the product as well. The course was a profoundly personal engagement as well, since I had the opportunity to reflect not only on course content but also on my entire educational history (parts that stood out any-way). For example, I had seen Kahoot quizzes used for me in a workshop unrelated to my schooling, and they had been a useful tool, and they eventually became part of the curriculum as a tool for the students taking the course. Dr. Yasira encouraged me to share new approaches and to explore technology in the classroom, and this freedom to experiment was one of the reasons that this partnership was so exciting.

A SPIRAL PARTNERSHIP: DISCUSSION, FEEDBACK,
OBSERVATION, REVISION . . . DISCUSSION, FEEDBACK,
OBSERVATION, REVISION . . .

Yasira: Our partnership unfolded in a unique way primarily because Moeed had been a former student in my course. We decided in our initial meeting in the summer that new pedagogical approaches needed to be introduced to increase student participation and engagement. Our focus was on reorganizing course material so that students learn to organize knowledge, and it is more meaningful in introducing new pedagogical approaches to keep the students actively engaged. A similar approach was used by Bunnell and Bernstein (2014), who included students in course design and found that after incorporating three chapters from the book suggested by students and a 6-minute interview to introduce the readings, student engagement increased with the topic. In their course redesign experience with students, Mihans et al. (2008) also included the core textbook, interactive media, supplemental material-articles, videos, and tasks that were recommended by student collaborators. Moeed and I felt in good company in our course redesign process.

In our first weekly meeting, Moeed suggested that the first part of chapter 1 could be skipped as the topics of this chapter are never used again in the course. We discussed how the course content could get covered without these additional topics and deleted the topics. For each week, as our meetings progressed in the summer, Moeed also introduced short videos related to the course material that presented the content in an interesting way. It was interesting having a student as a partner from another school and discipline, as he shared specific learning experiences from his other course work, which I appreciated because they were not used by faculty in my discipline and I had not experienced them as a student. For instance, we decided to use Kahoot to gauge student understanding. The responses would be shared with students, and questions would cover common misconceptions. Moeed also shared a link where students could ask questions during the class, but the name of the student is not displayed, and a slide was added in class presentations for this purpose.

We also decided to have a closed group Facebook page for class participation as Moeed had used this in some classes. We developed a rubric for student participation in Facebook. Bunnell and Bernstein (2014), in their research on students as partners in course redesign, also discovered that the use of out of class technologies improved significantly after incorporating student feedback. Charkoudian et al. (2015) found as well that when students were co-designers of, for instance blog prompts, the quality of student writing improved.

Moeed: We took up the outline of the course as a living document, and in each meeting we had in the summer, we would reflect on the outline of the course, discuss course content and essential questions for the week, and share audiovisual resources that could be used in the course. This process continued beyond the revision stages into the semester, where we would change activities to improve student understanding as the course was unfolding.

One of my suggestions during the summer re-designing phase was to take out some extra topics that came once or were topics only vaguely authentic in the Pakistani context. To my surprise Dr. Yasira agreed and told me she wanted herself to resequence portions of the course to introduce them in a way that enhances understanding. One way we did this was to make the first week of the course more generalizable. The content in the first week would introduce fundamental concepts that would recur in the course as we would progress. I was initially surprised by the level of autonomy I was granted in these revision processes; it gave me room to experiment with what I had learned in the course. After our initial discussion, Dr. Yasira encouraged me to introduce graded instruments and student experiences that I felt might lead to more generative experiences in the course.

Two examples illustrate this autonomy. I introduced clicker-based pre- and post-assessment using Kahoot and an online collaborative reflective journal using Facebook. A lot of these instruments came from the synthesis of my college education and were based on reflection on what worked and what could have been better in my own learning. We decided in the summer that I would manage the Facebook group and students would write one reflection per week based on the readings and discussions done in the class. We decided to use Facebook for this course for multiple reasons: first, the learning curve for using Facebook would be low and would not need to be taught. In one of my courses with Dr. Yasira, Computer Problem Solving and Cooperative Learning, I had learned the benefits of online collaboration and thought Facebook could serve as a useful tool in asynchronous collaboration. This would also remove the pressure from students from participating in class-marked participation, allow them to reflect on their writing and their peers' writing, and potentially help shy students that do not contribute in the class discussions: these students should not be at a disadvantage.

During the implementation of the course, we saw the advantages unfold, but we also noticed certain disadvantages. For example, online participation was becoming onerous for some students, so we tweaked the policy early on by giving students the space to experiment by selecting only the top five graded entries for the final class participation grade and introducing in-class alternatives for students who wanted their participation to be in class rather than online.

In the summer, we mostly reflected on the content, and during the semester we focused more on pedagogy or approaches to be used in the classroom, and our weekly reflection was based on pedagogy and theory. Our partnership is built on mutual trust, where she trusts me to suggest a teaching approach for the classroom, and she invites me to reflect on the content of the course with her. I want to emphasize that the partnership never feels over-bearing. If I have an opinion on how something should be, it is given due consideration. If she says that something cannot be enacted, it is always communicated as a teachable moment. She will explain how what I am suggesting may not lead to what I intend it to by drawing on her experience and pedagogical knowledge.

I want to give a specific example of such a moment: a student asked me to accept his late class participation submitted on Facebook because of a mis-understanding of the course policy, and since I was managing class participa-tion, I was about to grant only this student an extension. Dr. Yasira told me that I could do anything so long as I made the option available to every student who had had a misunderstanding. While I realized the need for empa-thy and to keep students engaged in the education process, Dr. Yasira made the concept of fairness very clear. So, I decided against making an exception for a single student and made a public announcement on the learning man-agement system (LMS) that would be inclusive of all students. I defined, with Dr. Yasira, the scope of a misunderstanding and gave anyone with such a misunderstanding an opportunity to make another submission. With this exercise, I learned how I could remain fair to everyone while being accom-modating to students.

MUTUAL TRUST AND RESPECT

Yasira: One of the critical insights I gained through working with Moeed was that without this partnership I would never have thought deeply about my teaching practices or the content of the course. It is difficult for me to critically reflect on the course that I have designed myself, especially when the design process entails review of courses designed by experts and input from faculty in the department. All new courses are presented in the Aca-demic Committee meeting at the School of Education where faculty give input on course content and assessment practices. The course is presented again to the committee after incorporating the suggestions. It is only after stages of review that courses are offered.

Given this process of course development, it is difficult for the professor to assess the activities done in the class from the students' perspective, even if the desired outcomes are clear to the teacher designing the activities. The student as a co-designer, as Moeed and I developed the role, is a non-threat-ening partner in the learning process who is not a faculty member or a formal evaluator. He is a dialogue partner who offers informal feedback to help the teacher to reflect deeply. A similar feeling is shared by Charkoudian et al. (2015) in their course redesign process with former students: "I consciously created an environment of pedagogical transparency and fostered an environment in which students could come to me with continual feedback and suggestions to make the course stronger. . . . This experience taught me that the nexus between 'teacher's perspective' and 'students' perspective' creates fertile ground for learning."

In my course redesign process, the feedback was specific as it was grounded in observations that make it meaningful for me and hence it is also not taken negatively. The focus of feedback is the activity or the behavior and how it can be improved, rather than on me as a teacher. What helped our partnership the most was trust and respect. I trusted Moeed's suggestions and feedback, and there was mutual respect for honest feedback. Moeed did give me some push back on course content and activities, but it was always with respect. Having a candid dialogue with someone who is also an observer and putting in effort to improve my teaching were unintended outcomes of this initiative. Bunnell and Bernstein (2014) also share similar feelings of the teacher in their course redesign experience. Having an observer (Moeed) just made me more conscious of my pedagogical approaches especially when he is also aware of the course content. Moeed was in every class, so it was very different from sporadic observations where the faculty may plan an extraordinary lesson for one day. Moeed and I could see changes over an extended period while keeping in retrospect the way the course was taught previously.

Informal engagement with the student partner turned into a formal reflection and dialogue as we progressed through the course. I learned that if I push myself, I can further improve my current teaching practices. The collaboration forced me to think deeply about issues I tend to ignore in the rush when the semester starts, for instance, activities to be done by students to facilitate learning get pushed back when the semester starts. Moeed helped me to remember to prioritize content alongside engaging learning activities.

The partnership affirmed that teaching is a continuous spiral process that needs revisions to make learning engaging and to enhance the teaching and learning experience. It is also these reflections and dialogue that make the course come alive for both the students and the teacher. We followed the cyclical process of having discussions on course structure and content, incorporating feedback to revise the course, conducting observations in the class, and then further revising after observations.

Moeed: Through this partnership I discovered that I was passionate about developing learning experiences that could transfer knowledge in the most instructive way. For me learning about new ways to engage the classroom was exciting, and I would want to try it out in the classroom when given the opportunity, such as introducing the use of Kahoot. I started thinking about teaching and learning in a completely new way, maybe because I started developing a vocabulary and a practical understanding of it. Teaching and learning were about the design of learning to facilitate students developing an understanding of the content of the course and applying what they learned in different contexts.

It was exciting to be a part of this new kind of collaboration with a professor, where as a student I was not doing the tasks directed by the professor but rather I was a part of the selection of tasks. I was having dialogue as an equal, not as someone seeking advice or directions from the professor, which is a very different experience. This partnership developed my interest in teaching. One student in the research of Charkoudian et al. (2015) expressed similar feelings on working as co-designer.

I learned that the process of coming up with a rewarding and fulfilling educational experience can be a challenging task that needs a lot of attention. There are always ways to make the learning experience more instructive, and there are many ways to teach a difficult topic. Developing engaging and rewarding activities that lead to substantial learning is a time-consuming, iterative process and requires a lot of working hours but is worth the effort.

I also realized that the teaching experience must be viewed as a science and as a way of thinking. For example, I began to see the role of the teacher with the students in a new light. The teacher is responsible for an account-able, safe space in the classroom. If there is a sense of favoritism, it can upend the learning experience for students. Therefore, policies need to be thought out and then strictly enforced.

ADVICE

Yasira: This partnership was productive because I was open to criticism. It may be uncomfortable in the beginning as university faculty are not used to students observing their classes to share feedback, but it's also a rare oppor-tunity to have. A challenge for the new person entering this relationship can be in the establishment of mutual trust and respect, where candid feedback can be given and taken with respect. I got used to observations as Moeed was there in every class session, so duration of time is also important.

I am not sure if it's possible in every context, but assigning some minor role to the student observer wherever possible in conducting some class activities may also help in establishing a good relationship between the ob-server and the teacher. The purpose of the observer then changes from solely being on the student side to being a facilitator with the teacher.

Moeed: I'm not sure if such a partnership is possible with other instruc-tors because they might not feel comfortable with giving a student the level of autonomy Dr. Yasira granted me. I'd recommend giving students some degree of autonomy to introduce new methods or to axe old ones, because that may help student partners be more candid in their feedback and encour-age them to participate fully. If Dr. Yasira had told me that certain things are just not possible to change, then I would have never given any feedback or suggestions in those areas, or if I had felt that she was uncomfortable with me suggesting changes, even that would have been discouraging.

I tried to approach the partnership with a learning mindset: setbacks are learning opportunities. If a class activity did not work the way it was intended to work, then that became a lesson on how not to conduct an activity. I found student feedback to be valuable, and for that, anonymous surveys work best because most students did not voice their opinions if directly asked.

Lastly, I found it essential to remind myself of the importance of what I was engaging in. There were rare moments that were dull in the summer during the designing phase, but the work payed off in the middle of the semester when I saw marked changes in the quality of student engagement in the classroom.

REFERENCES

Bunnell, S., & Bernstein, D. (2014). Improving engagement and learning through sharing course design with students: A multi-level case. *Teaching and Learning Together in Higher Education, 13*, http://repository.brynmawr.edu/tlthe/vol1/iss13/2

Charkoudian, L. K., Bitners, A. C., Bloch, N. B., & Nawal, S. (2015). Dynamic discussion and informed improvements: Student-led revision of first-semester organic chemistry. *Teaching and Learning Together in Higher Education*, 15, https://repository.brynmawr.edu/tlthe/vol1/iss15/5

Healey, M., Flint, A., & Harrington, K. (2016). Students as partners: Reflections on a conceptual model. *Teaching & Learning Inquiry, 4*(2), 1–13.

Mihans, R. J. II, Long, D. T., & Felten, P (2008). Power and expertise: Student-faculty collaboration in course design and the scholarship of teaching and learning. *International Journal for the Scholarship of Teaching and Learning*, 2(2), Article 16.

Chapter Nine

Learning through Cooperation

Interdisciplinary Insights into Students' Experiences in a Developing Program

Katie Quy, Ashly Fuller, Ayushi Kar, Miyama Tada Baldwin, and Omar Hallab

CONTEXT

Provided by Dr. Nick Grindle, Senior Teaching Fellow, and Abbie King, UCL ChangeMakers Manager, UCL Centre for Advancing Learning and Teaching (CALT).

University College London (UCL) is a research-intensive university with its main campus in central London. At the time of this writing, it has just over 40,000 students, divided between undergraduate, postgraduate, and research by an approximate ratio of 13:11:4, and about 7,500 academic staff (faculty). Almost half of UCL's students come to London to study from outside the UK.

UCL ChangeMakers is a centrally funded initiative to support student-staff partnership work in the shape of educational enhancement projects. UCL is committed to working with its students as partners, and has been working towards involvement of students in all aspects of quality assurance and enhancement. UCL ChangeMakers is one example of that commitment. Running since 2014, the scheme has grown to support 64 projects in 2017/ 18. Until 2019, teams would apply to the scheme and funding was awarded by student/staff panels. Proposals were judged on their likelihood of making an impact, how students and staff would be working in partnership with each other, and the alignment of the project with institutional priorities. Going forward, this process will change slightly, as partnership projects will be instigated through staff-student consultative committees (SSCCs) and approved at the departmental level, thereby encouraging departments to think about the ways students can meaningfully be involved in enhancement work, as opposed to superficial student representation.

A NOTE ON WRITING THIS CHAPTER

When writing this chapter, the team felt that the most appropriate approach would be, in the spirit of partnership, to write collaboratively, with the exception of the project background and introduction. This approach has allowed us to write about the partnership from a broader perspective, as a team, rather than as individuals. On occasion, direct quotes have been included to illustrate particular points or demonstrate individual insights, and these have been attributed to individual team members.

EMBARKING ON PEDAGOGICAL PARTNERSHIP: INTRODUCTION BY DR. KATIE QUY

When the idea for this project first came about, the first year of the Department's new undergraduate Social Sciences program was coming to an end. I was reflecting on my experiences over that time and the different perspectives my various positions afforded me: as Admissions Tutor, meeting applicants and potential students and their families as they made decisions about where and what to study; as a lecturer teaching in a new and rapidly developing degree program; and as a personal tutor, meeting with young people just starting out in their academic careers. The program was in an exciting position, developing a promising new interdisciplinary Social Sciences degree, and engaging with complex social issues through the multiple lenses of social science. As a department, we were building a program that aimed to provide our students with a globally relevant, evidence-based, and research-led education, equipping them to become social scientists of the future. I saw an opportunity to draw on our early experiences to enrich the program and ensure that it was best tailored to the needs of our students.

As part of this process, there was a place to include student voices in shaping the program. I hoped that a partnership approach would help access multiple perspectives, which could give us a deeper understanding of how we might continue to develop the program (Cook-Sather & Abbot, 2016). The project I proposed was designed to have two main strands: an evidence focus, designed to gain a better understanding of student perspectives on an interdisciplinary degree with a global outlook, and an enhancement focus, designed to maximize program relevance and quality. In order to achieve these goals in a meaningful way, we needed to work in partnership with our students in a way that engaged them as equal or even lead contributors, rather than merely engaging token involvement (Delpish et al., 2010).

In my initial thinking about how such a partnership project might unfold, I drew heavily on UCL's Connected Curriculum framework (Fung & Brent, 2017). This is an institution-wide initiative that aims to ensure that all students are able to learn through participating in research and inquiry at all levels of their program of study.

I was primarily inspired by two Connected Curriculum Dimensions:

Dimension 4: Programs give students the chance to connect academic learning with wider learning and skills; for example, teamwork, project management, creativity, enterprise and leadership. Students become increasingly aware that they are developing a rich range of understandings, skills, values, and attributes to take into their professional lives, and are able to articulate these.

Dimension 6: Students often value greatly a sense of belonging, of being part of a learning community. This sense of community can be enhanced in a number of ways: through team-based activities or group projects; through small group tutorials led by an academic tutor or personal tutor; and through engaging with one another across phases of study and with alumni, for example through peer mentoring.

The idea was to engage students in aspects of curriculum planning and development, with the aim of their taking ownership of their learning and degree trajectory and helping to shape their program of study.

I also hoped that the project could provide opportunities for teaching staff to develop their practice and broaden the curriculum to ensure the interests and needs of the students were being met.

DEVELOPMENT OF THE PARTNERSHIP

The first step in launching the project was to secure departmental buy-in, which was facilitated by the program leader who was supportive from the outset, and keen to promote the initiative. She was also key in ensuring the project would be sustainable from a practical perspective; without her collaboration, no partnership could be a meaningful agent for change.

The next step was to recruit student partners. All students from the department were invited to an open meeting to explain the scheme and explore the shape this kind of project might take. It was also important at this stage for us to set some boundaries around what the project was *not*. For example, it was important to ensure that we would not overlap with or replicate existing roles and structures, such as student representatives. Students interested in joining the team were invited to submit their thoughts on what a student advisory board might look like, and the role it might fulfill. Based on the ideas they submitted, the student partners (and authors of this chapter) were asked to join the core project team.

The team agreed that the main objective for the project should be to establish a student advisory board to feed into the planning process and ensure student views were included. Our first tasks were to find ways to collect some data from the larger student body and think about the form that a student advisory board might take. We held regular, extensive meetings to discuss the different stages of the project, and decided that it would work best to employ a mixed-methods approach. In the first phase, we developed a survey for students, which explored student perspectives on subject interests, new module development, and post degree / career planning. In the second stage, we carried out focus groups to explore themes arising from the survey data. Having team members from across the department allowed for a rich exchange of knowledge and information on methodology and approaches. We were able to take into consideration, for example, subject backgrounds and experiences in methods training; some team members had greater experience in quantitative data analysis while others had qualitative research methods training. We also drew on skills developed through internships and work experience. A key strength of the team was our openness to sharing diverse experiences and backgrounds, from addressing the best way to frame questions in the survey, to 'how to run focus groups' etiquettes.

WORKING IN PARTNERSHIP

Working in partnership turned out to be a complex, but ultimately rewarding, experience. At the outset, it was a delicate negotiation between staff and student partners. From the staff perspective, it was sometimes difficult to relinquish the role of lecturer directing student activities. From the student perspective, there was a period of adjustment as student partners moved from viewing the project as a task—*"oh well it's a uni[versity] project, I've been selected, and I'm getting paid so I better get this done"(Ashly)*—to a change of mindset as the team developed a relationship that translated into a partnership with a growing commitment to the project and a stake in the outcomes.

Before joining the project, many members of the team were relatively unknown to one another. However, the weekly meetings and discussions of the project led to discovery of our group as a team: who was good at doing what, who had particular skills, the roles and functions that were assigned. Gradually, student partners started to take the lead in driving the project, deciding what we were planning to do, how, and when. This was a turning point in the partnership. Up to this point, the staff partner had provided the structure and guided the project throughout; but now the student partners were developing their agency, leading the way in setting out what we wanted to achieve.

> Participating in the project was for me an unexpectedly exciting and rewarding experience. I underline 'unexpected' here because I did not imagine at its beginnings that the project nor the people working on it, would impact me personally and academically.—Ashly, lead student partner

The process of working in a team was not without its difficulties. Undertaking this project alongside study commitments was a delicate balance, particularly for those of us in our final year. Deadlines would be set for reports to be drafted or data analyzed, but they would often have to be pushed back as assessments and dissertations took precedence. The freedom of being able to define the project and deadlines can be a double-edged sword; plans can rapidly fall into inaction if there is no organization. Drafting the first report became one of the most difficult moments for our team, but also an important turning point in our partnership with one another. One student partner would often be the first one to message the group, reminding the others of what had to be written or analyzed and prompting them to comment on the work she had done. There were concerns around 'overstepping' peers, or pressuring them toward taking on a greater share of the workload. However, these issues brought with them a new conception of partnership:

> I think it's at that moment I realized what a collaboration was: it's not doing the homework of someone else; it's trusting your peers would do the same for you if you couldn't.—Ashly, lead student partner

We started to adopt a new form of working together, less ruled by who *had* to do what, but rather by who was *good at* doing what. The driver of the project was not a top-down imperative of *having to do*, but rather an intrinsic motivation to accomplish. At the end of term, the student partners met to discuss communication in the next stage of the project and ask each other how it could be made more effective. Ashly voiced her concerns around overstepping the mark and taking control, but noted the need to keep in mind the work and realistic deadlines to be met. While the conversation was difficult, as other team members expressed feelings of guilt for letting others down, the culture of trust that had been established within the team, and the strong feelings of ownership about the project allowed us to move forward and find a solution. We decided to name one member 'lead student' of the project, in recognition of her contributions, and as a solution to the issues of communication.

INSIGHTS INTO LEARNING AND TEACHING THROUGH WORKING IN PARTNERSHIP

Working in partnership was an experience that enriched the whole team's approach to learning and teaching. Team outputs were shown to the department, and student partners were considered to be on an equal footing with faculty. Partnership meant relationships and interactions were horizontal rather than vertical. Staff and students were working to achieve a collective goal, for the team, for the department, and ultimately for future students.

An important component of both the ChangeMakers philosophy and of this project was the opportunity for student partners to lead research and apply the skills we had developed as part of our learning in a 'real-life' setting. We found that the application of in-class learning to a tangible and meaningful project was both empowering personally and useful academically.

> Such an opportunity has definitely put into perspective how relevant all that I had learned had been. . . . I kept referring to our project as a "Social Sciences Consultancy" because it really felt as if we were running a consultancy project for our own course.—Omar, student partner

Peer learning was also key. As students from interdisciplinary programs, with particular methodological perspectives, we afforded one another many opportunities for mutual learning and teaching within our group.

LESSONS FROM ENGAGING IN PARTNERSHIP

Important lessons from the partnership included reflections on enfranchisement, both for staff and students; how partnership can be a driving force for institutional change and reform; and individual self-reflection and learning.

Empowerment was a key theme arising from the partnership:

> We each raised issues that we had encountered . . . as well as our vision for the kind of educational experience we wanted our degree to be. On a personal level, this was very satisfying and empowering for me. . . . It was the first time I felt that I was contributing to finding a solution.—Miya, student partner

> I felt a sense of power conducting this project, because I was taking my university experience into my own hands, and helping those around me shape theirs too.—Omar, student partner

This feeling of empowerment allowed us to develop confidence in our own skills, and reflect on our strengths:

Being part of the UCL ChangeMakers team undoubtedly made me question, at every stage, how I can best benefit the team with my knowledge, experience, and exposure. I had to constantly reflect on my strengths and weaknesses, as well as learn new skills to continue working on the project.—Omar, student partner

The experience of being involved in a student-staff partnership has been extremely rewarding. It has given me the opportunity to develop and practice skills, such as research skills, team work, and time management, but also the chance to gain a different perspective on teaching.—Miya, student partner

Increased understanding of each side of the student/staff relationship was also important for us:

It was comforting to learn that we shared each other's concerns and commitment to find solutions, but also insightful to hear for the first time about these issues from a teaching perspective . . . ultimately working in a student-staff partnership led me to a deeper understanding of the opportunities to take ownership of my learning through collaborating with staff.—Miya, student partner

From a student perspective, the project was important as a meaningful platform for student voices, led by us as students. As Omar notes:

Having a student-led research project, meant that students' voices were front and center. We were researching a community that we were a part of, and cared deeply about.—Omar, student partner

We found that the insights we identified were also important for staff across the wider department: faculty were keen to engage with the findings of the project, and reflect on potential impacts on practice and the data we collated allowed us to present evidence-based recommendations. In June 2019, all students in the department were sent an email by the BSc Social Sciences program leaders, forwarding a document called *"You said, We did."* It highlighted issues raised by students and the steps taken by the department to fulfil these. Most of the issues raised by undergraduate students were topics and concerns that the ChangeMakers team had researched and presented to the department. We were very grateful and happy to see how our work had been taken into account and was already being acted upon in a meaningful way by higher levels of administration from our department.

Ultimately, we found the key to successful engagement in partnership to be communication. If communication is clearly settled and maintained throughout the project, then individuals and team members will be more likely to be honest, respectful, and attentive. While good relationships were an important aspect of maintaining a healthy work environment, it became clear to us that friendliness shouldn't override the clarity and honesty of communication.

The main challenge for our partnership was achieving a balance between keeping the group adhering to deadlines, and commitment to the project, with an unwillingness to impose hierarchies or take unwanted initiative. Communication within the team led to the proposal of a "lead student," as we noted earlier in our discussion, and communication was just as important in the staff/student partner relationship. When we had issues in meeting a deadline or accomplishing a task, instead of cramming or doing less, we could speak to the staff partner and tell her honestly, *"We need a bit more time."*

We also found that communication helped to preserve authenticity in the project:

> This project would not have been as successful if we didn't give our best and develop esteem in each other. I believe this project made us realize what a partnership was: a matter of trust. Whether it was Katie giving us full freedom and trusting us in the direction we decided to take with the project or within the team, we all contributed to this common project trusting each other.—Ashly, lead student partner

Though not without its challenges, the project was ultimately a highly rewarding experience for all of us. This was true from the perspective of the individual project goals, in terms of collecting data to inform program development, but, perhaps less foreseen, in terms of our individual growth, and developing new ways to think about staff and student roles. The aims of the original project were met, but also transformed by the inclusion of student partners as we took ownership of the project and produced something entirely new, learning a lot about both ourselves, and the program, in the process.

> Before this partnership, my perspective towards teaching was tinged with a sense of dissatisfaction, since all I saw were gaps which I perceived to be missed opportunities in my learning experience, and this created disillusionment that hindered my learning. [This project] made me understand the reasoning behind the present design of the course in the first place, and its utility.—Ayushi, student partner

> Without any doubt, if you ever get the opportunity to work on a student-staff collaborative project, definitely go for it. You will learn about your own student community, your educators, how you can improve the relationship between both, but you will also learn about yourself.—Omar, student partner

ADVICE TO OTHERS SEEKING TO
UNDERTAKE PARTNERSHIP WORK

We learned many lessons in the course of this collaboration. In the next section, we reflect on some of the key learnings that we have taken away from the project and how they might help others seeking to develop similar partnerships. One of the most important messages, though, is one of flexibility. Our partnership adapted and changed throughout the project in ways we did not anticipate at the outset. Allowing this to happen was not always easy, but ultimately worked. As Ayushi notes:

> I would advise to keep an open mind because often the result of such collaboration will even surprise you.—Ayushi, student partner

We would also advise partnerships ensure that partners feel capable of being open with one another. As Omar writes:

> Looking back, I think one piece of advice I would give is to just be honest with your team. Honesty is a key factor that can determine success in a project like this one. . . . It helped us organize our roles better and be on the same page.—Omar, student partner

As Ashly discovered, this might mean having some difficult conversations:

> Being honest was perhaps one of the main challenges for me... being honest meant accepting [both] my own and my peers' limitations. Being honest meant learning to say 'no' to unrealistic projections, and 'yes' to propositions I wasn't confident about.—Ashly, lead student partner

One of the biggest takeaways from our experience as part of our Changemakers project was that teamwork is the foundation of a successful student-staff partnership. This is because for our project all decisions were made collaboratively, and each member of the team contributed to its realization as a whole. For this reason, our advice to those who wish to undertake such partnership work is to focus on building team spirit and cultivating a rapport with each member. By being be able to rely on each other, we found our project was ultimately more successful and rewarding. This was particularly evident when it came to managing our time, as we had to carry out our project while also being busy full time students or, in the case of Dr. Quy, a university academic staff member. Working as a team meant that whenever other commitments arose, we could always count on each other for support and that our project could stay on track.

The time we took to engage with each other as a team and learn the strengths and weaknesses of each member was also key to ensuring the success of our project. This meant that we could each take on tasks that were most suited to our capabilities, leading to a more efficient distribution of the workload. For example, Ashly was the most organized, so she arranged our meetings, communicated with staff, and planned our agenda. Ayushi's more technical background in data science meant that she was most prepared to deal with the analytical components of our research. Ultimately, we understood how each member could best contribute by taking the time to engage with each other and come together as a team.

While working as a team can be a particularly rewarding experience, it also has its challenges. As each of us had busy schedules, finding time to meet, to discuss plans, and to implement our project was always problematic. For this reason, ensuring that there was clear communication between each member of our team was of paramount importance. Whenever there were any issues, we would raise them amongst ourselves and find a solution. This was possible because we prioritized creating a working relationship in which we felt comfortable relying on each other as a team.

For student partners, it is also important to have confidence in the value of your role. Taking on a partnership can be particularly intimidating for students, who are often unused to being in a position of power within the university dynamic. True partnership should ensure that staff and student partners are on an equal footing.

> Stand behind your opinions and your perspective of the project, since you are as important as your tutors and the purpose of such projects is to build understanding about both perspectives. . . . Cherish this as a positive experience in your academic journey!—Ayushi, student partner

A final point of advice to those wishing to undertake a student-staff partnership is to keep in mind that this kind of work is a great opportunity to practice many life skills. As Miya reflects:

> Being involved in a student staff partnership has been fundamental in the development of my teamwork, organizational, negotiation, research, writing and presentation skills, while having a tangible impact on shaping my educational experience and that of future Social Sciences BSc cohorts. For this reason, I recommend to everyone interested to engage in such a partnership, as it is a rewarding and enriching experience.—Miya, student partner

REFERENCES

Cook-Sather, A. & Abbot, S. (2016). Translating partnerships: How faculty-student collaboration in explorations of teaching and learning can transform perceptions, terms, and selves. *Teaching & Learning Inquiry, 4*(2). http://dx.doi.org/10.20343/teachlearninqu.4.2.5

Delpish, A., Darby, A., Holmes, A., Knight-McKenna, M., Mihans, R., King, C. and Felten, P. (2010). Equalizing student voices: Student-faculty partnership in course design. In: Werder,

C. and Otis, M.M. (eds.), *Engaging student voices in the study of teaching and learning.* Virginia: Stylus Publishing.

Fung, D. & Brent C. (2017). *UCL connected curriculum: Enhancing programmes of study.* Second edition. University College London, UK. Available online:www.ucl.ac.uk/connectedcurriculum

Chapter Ten

"With Your Basket of Knowledge and My Basket of Knowledge, the People Will Prosper"

*Learning and Leading in a
Student-Staff Partnership Program*

Ali Leota and Kathryn Sutherland

CONTEXT

Provided by Stephen Marshall, Director, Centre for Academic Development

Ako in Action is a student-staff partnership program co-conceived, designed, and coordinated by students and academic (faculty) developers at Victoria University of Wellington, a research-intensive university with about 22,000 students, in New Zealand's capital city. In 2017, the university introduced a new Learning and Teaching Strategy that embedded a bicultural approach to learning and teaching, built on the principle of 'akoranga.' Ako, the root word of this concept, is a Māori term that means both to teach *and* to learn, and is enacted at our university as a 'collective responsibility for learning.'

Looking to deepen this university-wide commitment to akoranga, the Centre for Academic Development (CAD) instigated a pilot partnership program in 2018, undertaken by six students and six faculty members (including four associate deans and two junior academics). Throughout the pilot, students partnered with academics to observe their teaching and consult on course design, followed by reflective conversations that drew out possibilities for change and enhancement. Over ten weeks, students attended weekly meetings at CAD, co-coordinated by two academic developers and a senior student leader. Students learned about the university's learning and teaching values, the power of pedagogical partnerships, their own learning approaches and preferences, and how to listen actively and ask open questions. Participating academics engaged in reflective conversations with pairs of students after their lecture observations and attended a group meeting of all participants to reflect on the design and structure of the program. Students in the pilot received a scholarship for their contribution to both the pilot partnerships and the concurrent co-design of the full Ako in Action program, which we launched in 2019. The Vice Provost Academic and CAD are sponsoring the student scholarships for the ongoing program.

The reflections below are written by one of the academic developers and one of the student leaders involved in the co-design of Ako in Action. Rather than focusing on just one academic-student partnership, this chapter describes the thrills and challenges of wider partnership in designing and running a program that encourages collective responsibility for learning across the university.

THE INSPIRATION FOR ACTION

Kathryn: I began my academic career twenty years ago, as an academic developer (or faculty developer as the role is more commonly known in North America), with a primary focus on supporting early career academics/faculty. In the first ten years of my job, I had little interaction with undergraduate students, other than the student tutors who attended various training workshops I offered. That all changed after I spent six years as Associate Dean (Students, Learning and Teaching) in the university's biggest faculty. This role helped me realize how much learning is going unharnessed and uncelebrated between learners and teachers. Returning to CAD at the end of 2016, I was motivated to work much more directly with students. Creating programs and opportunities where teachers and students could learn from each other, and where academic developers could learn from everyone involved, was a primary goal. But, the ideas I could independently produce were limited in their conception, scope, and reach. This lack of clarity, it turns out, was a great way to approach the development of a partnership program, as it made me much more open to a true experience of 'ako.'

Ali: I started my post-secondary education journey training to be an electrician, but my voluntary work with a local high school led to a change of heart. As a proud Pacific young person, I wanted to help shift away from the deficits that surround Pacific people and other minority groups, and to help improve health and educational outcomes for all. So, I am now studying towards a Bachelor of Health degree. I have learnt that education is not only about acquiring knowledge; it is about drawing things out of people, whether that be purpose, meaning, or an opportunity. Having previously served as a student representative, my input often felt like a 'tick the box' exercise, where my opinion was welcomed only after the design process was already complete. I met Kathryn at a student representative awards ceremony at the university, and she offered me an opportunity to become a student partner, in a pilot program, Ako in Action. I saw this as an opportunity to share my learning experience, enhance my student representative role, and gain better insight into education processes and possibilities. Moreover, I could be uniquely positioned to serve the student community in a way that might enhance learning and teaching at the university, and where my voice was a valued part of the conversation from day one.

EMBEDDED IN VALUES: PUTTING AKORANGA INTO ACTION

Ako in Action emerged from another project on embedding civic engagement within our curricula (Lenihan-Ikin, et al., 2020). We mooted the idea of trialing a 'students as partners' program like ones we had heard about elsewhere, but firmly embedded in the local New Zealand context. Fortunately, our university's new Learning and Teaching Strategy gave us a mandate to forge ahead. The Strategy's values draw from Te Tiriti o Waitangi (the Treaty of Waitangi) and represent New Zealand's, and our university's, commitment to partnership, with akoranga at the core. The five other values in the Strategy also lend themselves to the co-construction of reflective, collaborative, and dialogic teaching and learning experiences and they resonate beautifully with what we hoped to achieve through Ako in Action. During the pilot phase, we agreed to embed the program around these values, outlined in table 10.1. (NB: the translations in parentheses following the Māori words are how our university has interpreted these words for our context, not necessarily direct translations of how the concepts are used in everyday life.)

In Ako in Action, we ask *everyone* participating to think of themselves in partnership; it is not just *students* as partners, but also *academics* as partners and *academic developers* as partners. Furthermore, by honoring students' participation through scholarships—rather than by paying them as employees—we allow them to retain their identities as students in the partnership.

Kathryn: During the co-design phase, we planned for the values outlined above to underpin the program, but it wasn't until the pilot phase that student partners pointed out these values could provide the thematic motivation and the *structure* for the program. Thus, our weekly sessions with Ako in Action students are now structured around a different value each week.

Ali: After one of my peers suggested we use the values of the Learning and Teaching Strategy more actively in the design of the program, I immediately pondered whether these values featured in my own learning experience

Values	Actions
Inspire *whai mātauranga* (intellectual curiosity) through reflective practice	—Support academics to seek student perspectives on their teaching —Increase students' awareness of teaching and reflection on their own learning processes
Embrace *whanaungatanga* (an extended family of collaborative learners) through collaboration between academics, students, and academic developers	—Develop meaningful and ongoing teaching-and-learning-focused interactions within and between students and academics —Welcome students more deliberately into the CAD whanau (extended family)
Develop *rangatiratanga* (autonomous learners and leaders) of teaching and learning	—Develop student and academic champions of akoranga —Encourage leadership in the scholarship of teaching and learning —Give students and academics new entries for CVs, promotion/award/job applications
Demonstrate *manaakitanga* (the generous fostering of knowledge) through our learning and teaching practices	—Develop empathy for each other's experience —Provide academics with iterative, regular, just-in-time, informal student perspectives on teaching —Encourage an ongoing reflective dialogue between learners and teachers
Foster *kaitiakitanga* (the guardianship of knowledge and wellbeing) by respecting and protecting the interests of participants	—Acknowledge and mitigate risks associated with participation in the program

at university so far, and if my current and past lecturers fostered them in their course design and teaching. It was inspiring to realize that some of them did. For example, in my Te Reo Māori language course, lectures were not held in a traditional auditorium; instead, they occurred in the university's *marae* – a sacred and communal space of Māori where their language and culture are celebrated and nurtured, and where students and teachers are surrounded by beautiful carvings, artwork, and visible reminders of the ancestors whose words resonate in our learning. In another course, my lecturer used a flipped-class model, where I retrospectively recognized the value of *rangatiratanga* at play, as students were given responsibility to lead the class in discussion rather than having to rely on the lecturer's lead.

I was able to take these positive examples of the values in action into my partnerships. When it came to observing one of my academic partners, my fellow student partner and I were able to commend her for already embracing *manaakitanga* in her teaching, as she provided printed lecture slides for students to annotate, rather than having to copy notes word-for-word. We also observed that she could build in more opportunities for her students to contribute to class discussion. In the first lecture we observed, she had only posed questions to the few students who were often vocal. During our reflective conversation, we suggested that she could introduce a one-minute discussion with neighboring students, a technique used in one of my courses that I had always found effective. It was amazing to observe her next lecture and see her trying out the suggestions we had made: more students spoke up because she had created an environment that allowed new students to be comfortable in sharing in class discussion. She was doing a fantastic job at fostering *whanaungatanga* in her teaching.

DRIVEN BY VALUES: HOW THE CO-DESIGN OF AKO IN ACTION UNFOLDED

Kathryn: Throughout the pilot, my CAD colleague [Irina Elgort] and I met weekly with the six students who undertook trial observations and reflective conversations. The students also helped us design the program we eventually launched in 2019. Each group workshop during the pilot phase focused on a different aspect of the partnership process: the first meeting with an academic partner, for example, and what kinds of questions to ask; classroom observations, and what to look for when observing; learning and teaching design, and what underpins a well-designed course. We also had sessions on topics like how sleep affects learning, how people learn, and learning to listen. As mentioned, we have since rejigged the structure so each workshop focuses on a value, but many activities remain the same, including a moment of reflective writing in each session.

Early on, I wrote in one of my reflections how thrilled I was at the direction Ako in Action was heading with student partners' input. Their thinking was fresh, hopeful, and ultimately quite demanding—they had higher expectations for what Ako in Action could achieve than I did! The pilot participants wanted Ako in Action to enhance the teaching behaviors of academics *and* transform the teaching culture university wide. "Why aren't all lecturers recording their lectures, they asked? How can (or should) we encourage this? How do we get lecturers to engage more actively with their class reps? How do we encourage more active learning that isn't just 'busy work' in big lecture classes?" They believed that Ako in Action could assist with practical answers for such questions. Time will tell, but as we have grown to a program with more than 60 active participants in 2019, I'm quietly hoping that such transformation might actually be possible.

The students in the pilot also believed that *all* the partnership activities should be reciprocal. While we had developed some guidelines for student partners participating in the pilot, we did not have corresponding guidelines for the academic participants. Thankfully, Ali filled this gap, brilliantly, and far more effectively than I could have done.

Ali: For me, stepping up to this responsibility was about helping to foster *whai matauranga* by creating a resource to be left behind for the next Ako in Action cohort. Although we showcased *kaitiakitanga* to students with their own guidelines in the pilot to ensure they were safeguarded and felt supported, we had not done the same for our academic partners. Over the course of the entire pilot, academics did not have guidelines to refer to, which put a bit of pressure on Kathryn as some academics were unclear on the basic expectations.

This highlighted that we were not living up to a true partnership. Consequently, I took responsibility along with others to create academic guidelines to ensure we walked the talk and affirmed the principles of reciprocity or *akoranga*. Thanks to our five-minute reflective writing exercises, during our weekly Ako in Action sessions, creating the guidelines was straightforward. We drew on communal and individual reflections to adapt aspects of the student guidelines into a new document for the academic partners. I had special input, too, by making sure the guideline's design was eye-catching and included bilingual phrases and inspiring proverbs, and I feel I've left a positive legacy for future partners, students, and academics alike.

INSIGHTS ON PARTNERING FOR CO-DESIGN

This legacy approach has been important to both of us during the co-design of Ako in Action. Recognizing that students move on, role responsibilities shift, and funding changes, we want to leave an easily adaptable program with robust systems, processes, and resources for future partners. To this end, we have reflected on insights gained from our co-design partnership, in the hopes they might inspire and inform future student and academic development partnerships.

Kathryn: Two key insights for me are that 1) planning in partnership requires transparency and can take longer (but usually produces better results), and 2) equal partnership doesn't mean everyone plays the same role, but everyone should have the chance to try out different roles and to be heard.

By the end of the pilot, I was confident we had designed a robust program to launch in 2019, but I didn't know if it would get off the ground. Thankfully, two of the pilot six (including Ali) were not graduating and agreed to stay on for 2019 as student leaders to help us put Ako in Action into, well, action. Having deliberately recruited students and staff for the pilot from what our government describes as 'equity groups' (including students from Māori or

Pacific Island backgrounds), I hoped this diversity would continue. It has, with a diverse range of student participants in every cohort, thanks in large part to Ali's active recruitment efforts! This diversity came to the fore in just our second session of the year in 2019, when we supported each other through varying responses to the aftermath of the horrific mass shootings that occurred in Christchurch three days prior to our Week 2 group meeting.

The emotions of that whole week weighed heavily on me at our planning meeting for the next session. I reflected that I had dominated the Monday session more than usual, perhaps in an effort to contain the emotion everyone was feeling and keep us focused on Ako in Action, not just on the tragedy of the week prior. I noted that while we had engaged in some useful small group discussions, and that the student leaders had each facilitated one of those small groups, I had spent more time talking on Monday than I intended and I wanted to avoid that in future sessions. What transpired in our Thursday planning session, though, was that I blithely *continued* to dominate the conversation. In my stressed-out response to an emotional week, I made hurried plans with my academic development colleague for the next week's session, without seeking input from the student leaders. This led to a key insight: partnership requires more deliberate, thoughtful, and transparent planning to which all partners feel able to contribute.

I had learned during the pilot that we had to be very deliberate about creating obvious and inviting times and spaces for students' input to come through. Simply saying we valued their opinions and saw them as equal co-design partners was not sufficient when we had not yet earned their trust. We had to build in activities that drew out everyone's voices, even if this was in writing afterwards, not just in discussion during our sessions. Yet, months later on this planning Thursday, I had failed to ensure such equal space; it fell upon a courageous student partner to quietly ask at what I thought was the end of a quick planning meeting, "What can *we* do to help out with next week?" That question challenged me not to masquerade at partnership. It prompted a whole rethink of not just the following week, but the rest of the year's program. We decided then and there to build student-led activities into every Ako in Action group meeting. Ali describes more, below.

Ali: When my friend raised that question during the planning session, it opened the door for us to put 'ako' into action even more than we already had through the pilot phase. I had new insights during my lecture observation partnerships in the pilot, about just how much effort goes into creating a lively and informative lecture, where everyone involved leaves having learned something new. Seeing the academic developers plan the sessions for Ako in Action reinforced this—a lot of work goes on behind the scenes to put a learning experience together. In the planning session that Kathryn writes above, I realized that if Ako in Action was really going to be a partnership, we had to step up as student leaders to contribute to the weekly sessions in an innovative way and make it ours as well as CAD's. We have this saying in Samoan culture, '*the pathway to leadership is through service*,' and I saw that I could serve by taking on more responsibility during the weekly workshops, not just the planning sessions.

As Ako in Action is a values-based program, I offered to facilitate a session on the Ako in Action values. The following week I was up in front of the group, with the support of my fellow student partner explaining the meaning of each value and encouraging the group to share how they related to each one. I felt I did a good job of exposing my peers to concepts that many of them had not encountered before; they seemed attentive and receptive. However, in the reflective session immediately afterwards, students revealed that many found learning about all five values in one workshop was overwhelming. They thought the values should be treasured with quality time for them to deepen their understanding and share their new knowledge with each other. At our next planning session, we agreed as a team to restructure the second offering of Ako in Action in 2019 around this idea. Now, the weekly workshops for student partners are structured around a different value. For me, the greatest insight from this experience is that while everyone might not respond in the way we intend with teaching and learning, the unexpected responses can sometimes lead to deep and lasting impact. That, and team work is vital!

This insight into the power of collaborative efforts, also played out for me in another way. At the beginning of this partnership, I had felt a little concerned because of my previous experiences as a token student representative on a few boards. I was afraid Ako in Action was going to be another case where academics expected me to have all the answers on behalf of all the students, but that no one would really be listening. My Ako in Action partnerships initially made me feel out of my league as an undergraduate student helping guide an academic. Imagine how I then felt being asked to partner on the co-design of Ako in Action itself—that was a step even further. However, the openness of our planning sessions really helped me build confidence to suggest an idea for mitigating similar feelings of doubt amongst other student partners. I proposed having *two* students partner with an academic, rather than one. And that's just what we have done: all academics meet first with at least two students, both from different disciplines than the academic's own. The benefits of this are threefold: first, shyer students know they don't have to go into an initial consultation with an academic alone. Second, two students in reflective conversation with an academic can bounce ideas off each other to allow a good flow of discussion without the 'awkward silence' moment. Last, and perhaps most significantly for the partnership, it gives academics insights from two different students who each have varying experiences of learning and will notice different things in the classroom, in course design, and throughout the consultative and reflective conversations that follow.

ADVICE

In closing, together, we highlight three key pieces of advice from co-designing and co-leading a student-staff partnership program: pair up, match up, and reflect often.

First, pair up. As Ali hints at above, talking to a lecturer is a big deal for a lot of students. In fact, students in New Zealand universities seem a bit more reticent than students in other parts of the world. A recent student engagement survey revealed, for example, that students at our university are far less likely than students in American universities to ask or answer questions in lectures, contribute to class discussions, or communicate with the instructor outside of class. We believe that programs like Ako in Action can work towards encouraging more proactive and engaged learning behaviors. Inherent in the concept of *akoranga* is reciprocity, along with collaboration in *whanaungatanga*, and mutual respect in *manaakitanga*. New Zealanders like doing things together. So, one piece of advice is to think about how to create partnerships that include more than one student. Thanks to Ali's initiative, each of our partnerships sees an academic (or in some cases a teaching team), paired up with at least two students, both from different disciplines. The academic gains more than one student perspective during the reflective conversations, and the students are emboldened by the peer partnership.

Second, match up. When we realized that we had created resources (and expectations) for student partners but not for academics, we worked to rectify that by creating guidelines for academics to accompany our student guidelines. We encourage other programs to match up their resourcing, too: whatever you offer for, or expect of, student partners, consider for and of academic partners, too. The resources and expectations don't have to be exactly the same style, length or intensity, but if we truly expect partnership, then we should resource for that. For us, this means that the 2020 offerings of Ako in Action will see us offer more support (in the form of optional weekly gatherings) for the academic partners, to match up with the weekly support that students get. It won't be the same, but it will be equally available.

Third, reflect often. Building reflective activities into our program has helped all participants, including the academic developers! We all (students and academic developers) actively recorded our reflections through the pilot phase and the first full cohort, but when it came to the full program, we dialed back the expectations around reflection because we'd moved from planning into action. We wish we hadn't. We had lots of different activities for generating reflection in the first phases of Ako in Action, but reflection in action should apply beyond planning and pilot phases. Even making time at the beginning of a group meeting for five minutes of free writing on what we've all learned from the previous week's Ako in Action activities can open up more lively, informed, and deeper discussion than if we launch straight in to open talk. Make time in your own programs for reflection, no matter at what stage.

Akoranga—the reciprocity of learning and teaching—is real. We have so much to learn from each other and we encourage others to create opportunities for this reciprocal learning to occur. As the title of our chapter indicates, "Nāu te rourou, nāku te rourou, ka ora ai te iwi." This is a Māori *whakataukī* (proverb) that literally translates as "With your basket of food and my basket of food, the people will survive/prosper." We have adapted it as a *whakataukī* for Ako in Action to guide our approach to collaboration and we encourage you to take a similar approach—with everyone's contributions from their own and shared baskets of knowledge, we will all learn and prosper.

REFERENCE

Lenihan-Ikin, I., Olsen, B., Sutherland, K.A., Tennent, E., & Wilson, M. (2020). Partnership as a civic process. In L. Mercer-Mapstone & S. Abbot (Eds.), *The power of partnership: Students, staff, and faculty revolutionizing higher education*, 87–98. Center for Engaged Learning Open Access Series.

Chapter Eleven

Concluding Reflections on Building Courage, Confidence, and Capacity

Alison Cook-Sather and Chanelle Wilson

In this final chapter of the collection, we look back across the chapters co-authors have written and reflect on recurring emphases in the ten stories. These emphases offer a different way of thinking about how pedagogical partnerships both require and develop courage, confidence, and capacity. The chapter authors' stories throw into relief:

- the generative nature of having extended time and dedicated space to be in dialogue that builds trust;
- the importance of grappling with potential barriers, including power dynamics;
- what naming reveals and enables;
- the importance of affirming different sources and forms of expertise that partners, particularly student partners, bring;
- how partnership builds courage, confidence, and capacity in students; and
- how faculty carry the lessons from partnership into their practice as teachers, curriculum designers, and program developers.

Echoing the final component of each chapter in the collection, we conclude each section of this chapter with advice.

THE GENERATIVE NATURE OF HAVING EXTENDED TIME AND DEDICATED SPACE TO BE IN DIALOGUE THAT BUILDS TRUST

While, by definition, partners work together, we want to illuminate the nature of the collaboration. We want to emphasize in particular (as the authors

103

themselves highlight) the generative nature of having extended time and dedicated space to be in dialogue that builds trust—a key component of partnership work (Healey, Flint, & Harrington, 2014; Goldsmith, Hanscom, Throop, et al., 2017; Macfarlane, Dennison, Delly, et al., 2018).

Authors who comment on the early stages of their partnership work offer glimpses into how dialogue builds trust. For instance, faculty partner Amanda Peach writes: "When Ashley and I first met, my goal was vague in nature. I told Ashley that I wanted to be a better teacher. Ashley talked me through the process of defining that so that we could arrive at a goal that was actionable and measurable" (Peach & Ferrell, this volume). Faculty partner Amrita Kaur describes how she talked her partner through this clarification and goal setting: "In getting started with our partnership, my first meeting with Toh was focused on clarifying our roles, building reciprocity, and clarifying expected outcomes of the collaboration" (Kaur & Yong Bing, this volume). These initial moments of dialogue are not necessarily comfortable or easy, but they are essential to finding agreed-upon starting points as well as desired endpoints. As faculty partner Yasira Waqar explains:

> Although I had been excited about discussing my course with a student, the first meeting with Moeed was the most difficult, as I found myself feeling uncomfortable discussing possible improvements in the course with my former student. Admitting as a professor that there are weaknesses in the course that can be strengthened made me vulnerable in front of my student.
>
> Moeed had the outline of the course already with him, and he knew the readings. We started with a brief overview of the course, and then I told him that I wanted to revise the course during the summer as I was not happy with the last offering. Moeed agreed with me and said that he also thought certain aspects of the course could be improved. Our agreement put me at ease as both of us had a common goal to incorporate activities in the course. (Waqar & Asad, this volume)

"So begins the conversation," writes Dionna Jenkins, student partner, both framing her chapter co-authored with faculty partner Tina Wildhagen and signaling the ongoing, extended nature of the exchange that constituted the partnership. Similarly, as faculty partner Kim Jones suggests: "Our initial conversation really built the basis for our subsequent interactions. Even though we were accomplishing our goals, I also felt like I was just having a fun and intellectually challenging chat with a friend. The trust we established in that first conversation made it easy to bring up even difficult topics, and I looked forward to our weekly meetings" (Wildhagen & Jenkins, this volume). Student partner John Ho captures this process succinctly: "Trust was gradually built through dialogues" (Chen & Ho, this volume).

These glimpses into the process of building trust that chapter authors offer reflect what current research is revealing about the process of developing productive partnerships. For instance, in a preliminary report on the research they have conducted on their partnership program, Reynolds and Greene (2019) trace a transformation that unfolds over the course of partnership, from partners being separate and sometimes suspicious, or simply struggling with gaps between them, to being connected and more trusting. Student partner, Toh Yong Bing, captures what this looked like in his partnership with faculty partner Amrita Kaur:

> Though the discussion was a casual and informal sharing session, I reluctantly but sensitively voiced my opinions. I slowly went through my list of points one by one, and I skipped some that I felt were a bit too critical. I constructed my words carefully and tried to avoid saying anything meaningless or offensive. As we continued our discussion, I sensed Dr. Amrita's openness through attentive and positive responses. Because of the way she responded, I became more willing and courageous to share that more critical feedback that I had left out earlier. Eventually, through this process, I gained confidence. Dr. Amrita's willingness to hear let me speak my mind effortlessly and meaningfully. (Kaur & Yong Bing, this volume)

And in his chapter with student partner Iska Naaman, faculty partner Doron Narkiss explains:

> As our relationship developed and we came to trust each other's responses, I would occasionally discuss with Iska related situations in other classes, and consult with her, relying on her unique point of view, while she shared with me some of her teaching dilemmas, as well as her successes in her practice teaching in school. (Narkiss & Naaman, this volume)

Other student and faculty authors share similar insights. Student partner Amarachi Chukwu notes that: "The conversations we were having were fun, eye-opening, and interesting in themselves and were made even better by imagining students getting an opportunity to similarly engage with the topics we passionately discussed every week" (Chukwu & Jones, this volume). And faculty partner Amrita Kaur explains that, "During this collaborative process, Toh and I achieved a balance between traditional power and contemporary agency to function responsibly in each of our roles" (Kaur & Yong Bing, this volume).

Advice: That so many chapter authors note the importance and describe the slow and intentional process of building trust suggests that having extended time and dedicated space is critical to partnership work. Trust building cannot be rushed. The work is about building understanding and empathy as well as capacity to learn from different perspectives and even disagree, and it is about drawing on those qualities to engage in critical, compassionate analysis, affirmation, and revision. Skimming through the contents of this collection, one contributor, Doron Narkiss, noted "an understandable amount of attention given to hierarchy within the institutions." He offered both analysis and response that we embrace as a form of advice: "In rereading our contribution, I saw how dissimilar [my co-author] Iska's and my takes on the partnership were, yet how a spirit of critical inquiry linked us on this journey."

The "spirit of critical inquiry" embraced throughout the long-term, relationship-building work in which chapter authors engaged has unique potential, we suggest, to build the kinds of courage, confidence, and capacity co-authors describe. Therefore, our advice here echoes Cook-Sather, Bovill, and Felten (2014): "The structures and norms of higher education do not necessarily foster the kind of respect that makes student-faculty collaboration into genuine partnership work, so we urge you to take the time to nurture trust and respect" (p. 3).

THE IMPORTANCE OF GRAPPLING WITH POTENTIAL BARRIERS, INCLUDING POWER DYNAMICS

One of the threshold concepts to partnership that Cook-Sather, Bahti, and Ntem (2019) discuss is that partnership is about sharing power, not giving it up or taking it away. Power differentials are structured into roles and responsibilities in higher education, and therefore all participants in pedagogical partnership need to grapple with questions of power (Cates, Madigan, & Reitenauer, 2018; Kehler, Verwoord, & Smith, 2017; Mihans, Long, & Felten, 2008). However, perceiving partnership as giving or taking away power can be a barrier. Drawing on and building courage, confidence, and capacity necessarily require grappling with assumptions about and dynamics of power and position, but partnership need not be about giving or taking away power but rather reconceptualizing it as shared.

Faculty author Katie Quy and student authors Ashly Fuller, Ayushi Kar, Miyama Tada Baldwin, and Omar Hallab name this reality clearly:

> Working in partnership turned out to be a complex, but ultimately rewarding, experience. At the outset, it was a delicate negotiation between staff and student partners. From the staff perspective, it was sometimes difficult to relinquish the role of lecturer directing student activities. From the student perspective, there was a period of adjustment as student partners moved from viewing the project as a task—*"oh well it's a uni[versity] project, I've been selected, and I'm getting paid so I better get this done"(Ashly)*—to a change of mindset as the team developed a relationship that translated into a partnership with a growing commitment to the project and a stake in the outcomes. (Quy, Fuller Kar, Baldwin, & Hallab, this volume)

Linking to the theme of trust we discussed in the previous section, student partner Angela Gennocro and faculty partner John Straussberger explain what they see as essential to overcoming the barriers of ingrained biases and entrenched power dynamics:

> to overcome that challenge of ingrained biases and power differentials, as well as the reticence to offer and receive what could be critical feedback, we needed to establish a peer relationship based upon mutual respect. To establish this trusting relationship, we spent considerable time in many of the early meetings, while going over the notes produced as a result of the classroom observations, *feeling out* the personality and approach of the other partner. (Gennocro & Straussberger, this volume)

These reflections on power—the "delicate negotiation" Quy and her student partners note and the building "mutual respect" Gennocro and Straussberger describe—nurture the development of partnerships that complicate established power structures and afford both partners opportunities to contribute in meaningful and productive ways. As student partner Dionna Jenkins describes: "With combined power, we enhanced our individual strengths and our dedication to the work put before us, creating an impactful learning experience for students and one that gave us a deeper appreciation for the rewards and challenges of team work" (Wildhagen & Jenkins, this volume).

Faculty partner Kim Jones argues that "discussion of power is so important in partnership programs," and her student partner, Amarachi Chukwu explains that "the open conversation" they had "complicated the generally implicit teacher-student power dynamic as we both conceived ourselves as knowers and learners simultaneously in this scenario" (Chukwu & Jones, this volume). Chukwu and Jones (this volume) also suggest that interdisciplinarity "disrupts existing power dynamics and allows real learning from different perspectives on teaching and learning."

Advice: Matthews (2017) argues that nurturing "power-sharing relationships through dialogue and reflection" is one of the key components of partnership work. Over time, relationship-based, teaching-and-learning partnerships can overcome power dynamics that are inhibiting. We advise those undertaking partnership work to have explicit discussions of the power dynamics at play in their context, and the relationships within those, and to be intentional about working toward power sharing. As Cook-Sather, Bahti, & Ntem (2019) note, partnership is "not about erasing or eliminating power; it is about being intentional in how you understand and work with power as a shared dynamic."

WHAT NAMING REVEALS AND ENABLES

The power of naming is a theme across pedagogical partnership work (Cook-Sather et al., 2019; Healey et al., 2019; Singh, 2018), and here we consider particular forms of naming—use of proper names, use of "we" as opposed to "us and them," and voices and authorship within this volume's chapters.

The use of first and last names and titles is related to navigating the power dynamics we discussed in the previous section. To navigate what student partner Toh Yong Bing characterizes as "the hierarchy and power in my context," he used "Dr. Amrita"—rather than "Amrita," the first name of his faculty partner, or "Dr. Kaur" (Kaur & Yong Bing, this volume)—as a way of "untangling the power dynamics." Student partner Moeed Asad makes the same choice, calling his faculty partner, Yasira Waqar, "Dr. Yasira" (Waqar & Asad, this volume). The student partners who co-authored the chapters in this collection all had to consider how they addressed or referred to their faculty partners, in accordance with their contextual norms and cultural values, as well as within the tangle of power webs in which many in academia are entrenched.

Regardless of how student and faculty partners address one another, the dialogue in which they engage builds courage, confidence, and capacity through developing a "we." That "we" does not mean that everyone is the same. On the contrary, it is the differences that make partnership rich. But the sense of connection—built through relationship, through ongoing dialogue, over time—is shared. All stories presented in this volume share perspectives on a collaborative *experience*, but this does not imply that the contributors, though they worked together, approached or experienced the partnership in the same way. The various perspectives that partners hold, related to their positioning in the hierarchy, are essential to uncover and acknowledge, as we discuss in the previous section on power. What is important is the partnership serving as "the link"—the space to connect, to co-create, to contemplate, and to inquire critically.

The "we" plays out in different ways in how authors chose to use their voices and author their chapters. All chapters include contextual framing, offered either by the director of the partnership program that supported the particular partnership on which the chapter focused or by the chapter authors themselves. The majority of the chapters include sections alternating between voices of contributors, and some of these include sections that are both co-authored and alternating. These are effective ways to convey that partnership is both a shared and an individual experience. Quy et al. (this volume), however, write in their introduction: "the team felt that the most appropriate approach would be, in the spirit of partnership, to write collaboratively, with the exception of the project background and introduction." As with all partnership work, it is essential to honor this variety in what 'we" means to different participants and authors.

Advice: As you embark on partnership, consider the norms and cultural values of your particular context and of the partners involved, and settle on ways of naming participants that are both respectful of important norms and values and that facilitate partnership work. Like so much of partnership work, this will look different across different partnerships.

Furthermore, be aware of the *us-them* frame that tends to dominate in higher education (Singh, 2018) and that forces would-be partners—students and faculty—to approach courses, teaching practices, and program development with less courage to collaborate, less confidence to share meaningfully, and limited capacity to work toward understanding and building on each other's experiences. The hierarchical order can position faculty and students as parties that interact but maintain distance in respect for authoritative positions, a dynamic that can foster isolation and an air of competition. A *we* frame encourages investigating complexities and changing these dynamics, as chapters in this volume illuminate.

Finally, consider carefully how to ensure that all voices are heard and that authorship reflects partnership principles. Ask yourself questions such as: What story do you tell and in whose voice? Whose conceptual frames do you use in analysis and writing? and, How do you decide about author order? (Cook-Sather, 2019).

THE IMPORTANCE OF AFFIRMING DIFFERENT SOURCES AND FORMS OF EXPERTISE THAT PARTNERS, PARTICULARLY STUDENT PARTNERS, BRING

The definition of partnership we offered in our introduction emphasizes respect, reciprocity, and shared responsibility. In order to maximize the likelihood that partners will be able to enact these premises, it is essential to affirm the different sources and forms of expertise partners, particularly student partners, bring. Virtually all partners are clear that faculty bring disciplinary expertise and, in many cases, teaching experience. Students sometimes need more explicit reminders about the expertise they bring (Burke, 2013). As a former student partner, Miriam Pallant (2014), argues: "While colleges recognize students' excellence in academics, athletics, and arts, the term 'expert' is reserved for faculty, when, in fact, students are experts in one very critical area: the experience of learning" (p. 1).

The "experience of learning" that constitutes one form of students' expertise can take several forms. One of these is the beneficial insight student partners can offer from the non-enrolled student perspective. Student partner Dionna Jenkins explains: "My role as a student partner, but not being a student in the class, put me in an interesting position . . . to hear and perceive course students' thoughts through an analytical lens, while at the same time being able to empathize and connect their experiences to my own" (Wildhagen & Jenkins, this volume).

Alternatively, students can bring the unique perspective and different form of expertise based on having completed the course or program under exploration. Faculty partner Yasira Waqar explains regarding her student partner, Moeeb Asad, that, "since he had taken this course, I was positive that as a former student he would bring valuable insights" (Waqar & Asad, this volume). Although uncertain of this himself at first, Asad did gain confidence and capacity through the partnership work:

> One of my suggestions during the summer redesigning phase was to take out some extra topics that just come up once or were topics only vaguely authentic to the Pakistani context and hence were not an integral part of the course. To my surprise Dr. Yasira agreed and told me she wanted herself to resequence portions of the course to introduce them in a way that enhances understanding (Waqar & Asad, this volume).

John Ho was more confident in the value of his perspective. His faculty partner, Julie Chen, explains:

> I recall meeting John at the end of his first year of study when he requested to meet in order to give feedback on the first year [medical humanities] curriculum. While he was very diplomatic in pointing out the strengths of the curriculum, he was much more passionate when he drew on his personal experience to advocate for a curriculum that focused more on 'practical medical humanities.' (Chen & Ho, this volume)

A third particular perspective students can bring, whether or not they have taken a course, is their lived experiences as students with particular identities. Faculty partner Amrita Kaur explains:

> Toh, being from a minority community in Malaysia, was able to draw my attention to the importance of highlighting the social differences in Malaysian society and ways to handle those differences through educational initiatives. Malaysia is a multi-racial society, which comprises three major ethnic groups—Malays, Chinese, and Indians. The three of them share different cultural and religious values; however, they often seek ways to enhance social cohesion. Toh recommended that I use this course as a platform to appreciate those differences. (Kaur & Yong Bing, this volume)

The different sources of expertise faculty and student partners bring inform differences of perspective and sometimes opinion, and these differences need not be impediments. As Julie Chen and John Ho suggest, partners can "agree to disagree, for the partnership calls upon ideals that are greater than the people themselves" (Chen & Ho, this volume). Indeed, as noted above and elsewhere (Abbot & Cook-Sather, 2020), differences of perspective, and even disagreements, are what make partnership rich and generative. Dionna

Jenkins and Tina Wildhagen take this as the premise of their chapter and partnership and articulate it this way:

> Differences between students and teachers need not function as impediments to fruitful teaching and learning experiences. Instead, differences can reveal opportunities for teachers and students to learn from each other. In this chapter, we reflect on some ways in which our differences manifested in the partnership and how we tried to use them to improve the teaching and learning experience for everyone. (Wildhagen & Jenkins, this volume)

Authors also note this generative potential in looking back at their chapters. For instance, faculty partner Doron Narkiss writes:

> Rereading our interleaved responses, it strikes me how differently we envisioned our process from the outset, how distinct our expectations, experiences, and responses were as well. Thus the dialogue between us in this chapter only gestures towards our long talks but does not fully reflect them in either form or content. Yet the critical momentum set up by the partnership has led both of us to return to the starting point of the process and to learn from it, not as repetition merely, but as a creative and learned re-vision. This re-vision is based on reflection and leads to change—to the voicing of needs, the discussion of alternatives, trial and error, and occasionally to some solutions. It is a never-ending process—all the more reason it should always be celebrated. (Narkiss & Naaman, this volume)

Advice: All faculty and student partners have essential insights, both thoughts and feelings, that, when recognized as expertise, can inform pedagogical development and revision. Recognizing and affirming faculty expertise can help assuage the uncertainties about sharing power and responsibility that some faculty bring to partnership, and having their perspectives affirmed by their faculty partners can help student partners build confidence and capacity (Cook-Sather, Bahti, & Ntem, 2019). We, therefore, recommend that faculty and student partners be intentional about inviting and affirming the different sources and forms of expertise that partners bring, paying particular attention to affirming student expertise, since that is less likely to be recognized or named.

HOW PARTNERSHIP BUILDS COURAGE, CONFIDENCE, AND CAPACITY IN STUDENTS

Like student partners in so many other stories of partnership (Abbott, 2016; Ntem, 2016; Perez-Putnam, 2016), confidence (Mercer-Mapstone, Dvorakova, & Matthews, et al., 2017), and capacity (Cook-Sather, 2011; Cook-Sather, Bahti, & Ntem, 2019), student authors of these chapters note the ways in which working in partnership builds their courage.

Echoing points from previous sections on building trust through relationship and acknowledging expertise, student partner Dionna Jenkins describes a process through which virtually all student partners move from uncertainty to greater courage, confidence, and capacity:

> Self-doubt is not uncommon at a place like Smith [College], but only when one has the patience with oneself to recognize this feeling and work through it can the most rewarding aspects of partnership be realized. It was counterproductive for me to dwell in thoughts of inadequacy. Tina and I think differently not only because of our different positions as professor and student, but also because we are different people. Embracing our differences helped me overcome my discomfort and begin to trust myself to be the "expert" in the room just as much as I trusted Tina. (Wildhagen & Jenkins, this volume)

Student partner Amarachi Chukwu also names the way that the partnership catalyzed this revision of herself: "The partnership was a transformational point for me in transitioning from seeing myself as a student whose role is to absorb knowledge from teachers/professors who hold all the knowledge, to envisioning myself as knowledge holder and producer" (Chukwu & Jones, this volume).

Other student authors note the ways that partnership helped them develop greater courage, confidence, and capacity, as students, future teachers, scholars, and leaders. For instance, about how partnership enhanced his capacities as a student, Toh Yong Bing writes:

> My partnership with Dr. Amrita also improved my experience and practice as a student. It has provided me an opportunity to assume a more proactive and critical role in reflecting on what I have learned and hence made me more accountable and conscious of my learning. I believe that it has enhanced my metacognition and self-regulation for my learning. I can now think more clearly about the learning process, and I can plan it more effectively. The partnership has taught me to view myself differently. The active process of viewing teaching and learning through a critical lens greatly influenced the way I view my relationship with the course, the teacher, and the students. . . . As a result of participating in this partnership with Dr. Amrita, I have found myself taking more proactive roles in the learning of another course and making connections. I have become more courageous in sharing critical thoughts, asking challenging questions, and creating discussion forums with ease. (Kaur & Yong Bing, this volume)

Regarding the ways partnership can inform student partners' futures as teachers, student partner Iska Naaman explains:

> I was also exposed to new teaching methods in Doron's lessons that I anticipate implementing in my own lessons. I started looking differently at the lessons of my other teachers. The most significant tool I received from the

project is critical thinking. I have stopped taking my teachers' methods for granted and started asking myself, and occasionally them, why they chose a particular method, did it fulfill what they set out to achieve, and if they were to teach the lesson again, what would they keep and what would they change? Before the project I would sit in class like a good student, summarize the lecturer's words, and do the assignments as required. I never thought why the lecturer gave this specific assignment, or why now, and what aims it fulfills. Sitting in class now, I see things from a lecturer's or teacher's point of view as well, and think about the practice of teaching, in addition to my experience as a learner. (Narkiss & Naaman, this volume)

About the ways in which partnership contributed to her courage, confidence, and capacity as a scholar, student partner Ashley Ferrell asserts:

So many amazing things have come from my involvement in this program. I had the opportunity to write and publish an article with Amanda. We then presented at a conference and hopefully convinced other librarians to follow in our footsteps. At Berea, there were two other librarian/student partnerships that came from our involvement. The most recent opportunity that has come from being involved in this program is the opportunity to write this piece. It has always been a goal of mine to write and present but I did not know how to get started. SFPP has given me the opportunity to complete my professional goals. (Peach & Ferrell, this volume)

And finally, student authors Miyama Tada Baldwin and Ali Leota write about the professional, leadership skills they developed through the partnership work. Baldwin writes:

Being involved in a student staff partnership has been fundamental in the development of my teamwork, organizational, negotiation, research, writing and presentation skills, while having a tangible impact on shaping my educational experience and that of future Social Sciences BSc cohorts. For this reason, I recommend to everyone interested to engage in such a partnership, as it is a rewarding and enriching experience. (Quy, Fuller Kar, Baldwin, & Hallab, this volume)

Leota reflects on taking up "the responsibility to work with a couple of others to create a set of academic guidelines to ensure that we were walking the talk and affirming the principles of reciprocity or *akoranga*" (Leota & Sutherland, this volume).

All of these are glimpses into how the personal and the professional intersect through, and as a result of, partnership. John Ho and Julie Chen offer an especially vivid example of this intersection in an assignment Chen developed for the medical humanities curriculum in the medical degree program at the University of Hong Kong (to submit "an annotated original photo that reflects the human experience of suffering and healing") that Ho took up, sharing the last photo he took of his mother in the hospital before she died and his "public letter in remembrance of her" (Chen and Ho, this volume). This is courage in curriculum, pedagogy, authorship, and the essence of relationship that underpins them all.

Advice: Because many students embark on partnership feeling uncertain and unconfident, it is important to create structures and opportunities for students to build their courage, confidence, and capacity through partnership and to note and name their growth. The regular meetings between and among student and faculty partners, regular meetings among student partners, and invitations to write about their work, as in these chapters, can all constitute such structures and opportunities. And while the partnership may be pushing the faculty partner to grow in the same ways as students, it is necessary for faculty to take the lead and affirm their student partners' contributions.

HOW FACULTY CARRY THE LESSONS FROM PARTNERSHIP INTO THEIR PRACTICE AS TEACHERS, CURRICULUM DESIGNERS, AND PROGRAM DEVELOPERS

Just as student partners carry lessons from partnership into their practice as learners (and sometimes teachers), faculty partners carry lessons from partnership into their classroom, curricular, and programmatic practices. Faculty partners in this volume write about this transfer in terms of how reflection informs their practice, including applying partnership principles in their own classrooms, being more transparent and explicit, and carrying forward the courage and capacity for further growth. They also talk about the influence of this work at the programmatic level.

Faculty partner Yasira Waqar writes: "One of the critical insights I gained through working with Moeed was that without this partnership I would never have thought deeply about my teaching practices or the content of the course" (Waqar & Asad, this volume). Tina Wildhagen offers another version of this point:

> Working in a pedagogical partnership has taught me that teaching alone does not necessarily invite active reflection during the semester. There are ways to reflect on one's teaching in real time when one is teaching a course alone, but teaching alone does not *require* this reflection. . . . Teaching in partnership changes the game. Active reflection is no longer an option that the teacher may take up as she wishes; it becomes a mandate (Wildhagen & Jenkins, this volume).

Wildhagen also explains how this work carries over into her teaching:

> What I have learned through working in partnership with Dionna is that active reflection introduces the possibility for teaching to become the thing that it

should be: an ongoing project between teachers and students, open to improvization, revision, and reflection. A beautiful thing happens in an effective partnership. Not only are the professor and student partners actively reflecting on teaching, but the students in the class begin to do so, as well. The students come to see themselves as partners in the project of the class rather than passive recipients of the material prepared by the professor. (Wildhagen & Jenkins, this volume)

Linking the partnership experience, with her student partner, to partnership she can imagine with students enrolled in her course, faculty partner Kim Jones writes: "Just as we had to build trust to make our partnership work, I will have to build trust with my students to facilitate open, honest discussion" (Chukwu & Jones, this volume).

Several faculty partners specify ways in which the partnership work made them more transparent and explicit in their teaching practice. For instance, John Straussberger explains that the partnership

had effects on my pedagogy that extended beyond the specific course on which we collaborated. In explaining my own rationale for assignments, activities, or practices in the course while talking with Angela, I came to realize the extensive benefits of transparency. . . . Since working with Angela, I have attempted to include more pedagogical transparency with students. I explain my rationale behind the meta-structure of the course as well as individual assignments, and the content- and skill-specific goals I hope students gain. (Gennocro & Straussberger, this volume)

Similarly, Doron Narkiss explains: "The partnership extended my teaching repertoire, making it more inclusive by spending more class time explaining, exemplifying, and ensuring understanding" and, in particular, was "instrumental in leading me to confront and reconsider not only the rationale of my pedagogical practice" (Narkiss & Naaman, this volume).

Finally, Amanda Peach sums up both changes in practice and changes in perspective that the partnership afforded her:

The changes Ashley and I implemented surpassed those modest hopes. We made several changes, big and small, the sum of which was the real gain: a sense of ownership over this new iteration of the one-shot lesson plan. This, in turn, fostered a renewed passion for work which had grown to feel rote and like an obligation more than anything. To feel a new and deeper connection to my work was a gift; the partnership process that got me there taught me that I am capable of growth and change, as well as confronting my fear. (Peach & Ferrell, this volume)

The kinds of changes in practice faculty carry away from the partnership can have program-wide impact as well. For instance, Katie Quy, Ashly Fuller, Ayushi Kar, Miyama Tada Baldwin, and Omar Hallab explain:

Working in partnership was an experience that enriched the whole team's approach to learning and teaching. Team outputs were shown to the department, and student partners were considered to be on an equal footing with faculty. Partnership meant relationships and interactions were horizontal rather than vertical. Staff and students were working to achieve a collective goal, for the team, for the department, and ultimately for future students. (Quy et al., this volume)

Similarly, Ali Leota and Kathryn Sutherland reflect:

During the co-design phase, we planned for the values outlined above to underpin the program, but it wasn't until the pilot phase that we realized— thanks to the suggestion of one of the student partners—that these values could not only provide the thematic motivation but also the *structure* for the Ako in Action program. Thus, our weekly sessions with Ako in Action students are now structured around a different value each week. (Leota & Sutherland, this volume)

Advice: Just as students need structures and opportunities to build their courage, confidence, and capacity through partnership and to note and name their growth, faculty, too, need such support. Depending on partnership program structures, faculty may or may not have the same kind of regular meetings to process their partnership work as student partners do, but we encourage faculty participants and program facilitators to create such spaces. We also encourage institutions of higher education to recognize partnership work in reviews of faculty, thereby legitimating and rewarding the courage, confidence, and capacity required for and built through partnership.

FINAL THOUGHTS

As these cross-cutting themes highlight, pedagogical partnership requires courage to undertake, and, in turn, it builds further courage alongside capacity and confidence. These chapters offer reflections on partnership work across contexts and in different stages of both individual and institutional development. There is a growing body of resources to support the deliberation involved in such work (Cook-Sather, Bahti, & Ntem, 2019; Healey & Healey, 2019; Mercer-Mapstone & Marie, 2019), and we hope there will also continue to be a growing body of stories that offer glimpses into the lived experiences of the work.

In her Foreword, Kelly Matthews suggests that we have opened up (another) space for dialogue—as partnerships themselves do and as this final chapter has attempted to reiterate. The variations and complexities across pedagogical partnerships and likewise, the stories people tell about partnership, whether through reports of empirical research, thought-provoking conceptual arguments, case studies, reflective essays, or other forms, need to make space for the variety of experiences and insights pedagogical partnerships generate and the possibilities they inspire in others. Just as Kelly brought curiosity to her read of this collection, we conclude this final chapter of this collection with curiosity regarding what stories may emerge next to capture the complexities of pedagogical partnership work.

REFERENCES

Abbot, S., & Cook-Sather, A. (2020). The generative power of pedagogical disagreements in classroom-focused student-faculty partnerships.

Abbott, C. (2016). Leaping and landing in brave spaces. *Teaching and Learning Together in Higher Education, 18.* https://repository.brynmawr.edu/tlthe/vol1/iss18/4

Burke, H. (2013). Legitimizing student expertise in student-faculty partnerships. *Teaching and Learning Together in Higher Education, 10.* http://repository.brynmawr.edu/tlthe/vol1/iss10/6

Cates, R. M., Madigan, M. R., & Reitenauer, V. L. (2018). "Locations of possibility": Critical perspectives on partnership. *International Journal for Students as Partners, 2*(1), 33–46. https://doi.org/10.15173/ijsap.v2i1.3341

Cook-Sather, A. (September, 2019). "Naming and navigating complexities: The challenges of inclusion and power dynamics in planning for, participating in, and publishing about partnership." University of Surrey, England.

Cook-Sather, A. (2011). Layered learning: Student consultants deepening classroom and life lessons. *Educational Action Research, 19*(1), 41–57.

Cook-Sather, A., Bahti, M., & Ntem, A. (2019). *Pedagogical partnerships: A how-to guide for faculty, students, and academic developers in higher education.* Elon University Center for Engaged Teaching Open Access Series. https://www.centerforengagedlearning.org/books/pedagogical-partnerships/

Goldsmith, M., Hanscom, M., Throop, S. A., & Young, C. (2017). Growing student-faculty partnerships at Ursinus College: A brief history in dialogue. *International Journal for Students as Partners, 1*(2). https://doi.org/10.15173/ijsap.v1i2.3075

Healey, M. & Healey R. L. (2019). Students as partners guide: Student engagement through partnership York: Advance HE

Healey, R. L., Lerczak, A., Welsh, K., & France, D. (2019). By any other name? The impacts of differing assumptions, expectations, and misconceptions in bringing about resistance to staff-student partnership. *International Journal for Students as Partners, 3*(1), 106–122. https://doi.org/10.15173/ijsap.v3i1.3550

Kehler, A., Verwoord, R., & Smith, H. (2017). We are the process: Reflections on the underestimation of power in students as partners in practice. *International Journal for Students As Partners, 1* (1). https://doi.org/10.15173/ijsap.v1i1.3176

Macfarlane, K., Dennison, J., Delly, P., & Mitric, D. (2018). Sailing through a storm: The importance of dialogue in student partnerships. *International Journal for Students as Partners, 2*(2), 144–150. https://doi.org/10.15173/ijsap.v2i2.3457

Mathrani, S., & Cook-Sather, A. (2020). Discerning growth: Tracing rhizomatic development through pedagogical partnerships. In S. Abbot & L. Mercer-Mapstone (Eds.). *The Power of Student-Staff Partnership: Revolutionizing Higher Education.* Elon University Center for Engaged Learning Open-Access Series.

Mercer-Mapstone, L., Dvorakova, S. L., Matthews, K. E., Abbot, S., Cheng, B., Felten, P., Knorr, K., Marquis, E., Shammas, R., & Swaim, K. (2017). A systematic literature review of students as partners in higher education. *International Journal of Students as Partners, 1*(1), 1–23.

Mercer-Mapstone, L., & Marie, J. (2019). Practical Guide: Scaling up student-staff partner-ships in higher education. Institute for Academic Development: University of Edinburgh. bit.ly/2EfUR16

Mihans, R., Long, D., & Felten, P. (2008). Power and expertise: Student-faculty collaboration in course design and the scholarship of teaching and learning. *International Journal for the Scholarship of Teaching and Learning, 2*(2), Article 16. https://doi.org/10.20429/ij-sotl.2008.020216

Ntem, A. (2016). Learning to be brave within and beyond partnership. *Teaching and Learning Together in Higher Education,18*. http://repository.brynmawr.edu/tlthe/vol1/iss18/6

Pallant, M. (2014). The dynamics of expertise. *Teaching and Learning Together in Higher Education, 11*. http://repository.brynmawr.edu/tlthe/vol1/iss11/2

Perez-Putnam, M. M. (2016). Belonging and brave space as hope for personal and institutional inclusion. *Teaching and Learning Together in Higher Education, 18*. https://repository.brynmawr.edu/tlthe/vol1/iss18/2

Singh, M. (2018). Moving from "us vs. them" to "us" through working in pedagogical partner-ship. *Teaching and Learning Together in Higher Education, 23*. https://repository.brynmawr.edu/tlthe/vol1/iss23/5

Index

About the Contributors

Abdul Moeed Asad is a third-year computer science undergraduate at the Lahore University of Management Science (LUMS) Pakistan. After exploring courses in education, psychology, and human-computer interaction, he developed an interest in leveraging learning theory in technology to produce more generative user experiences. He is currently also the president of the student society, Better Educational Engagement at LUMS.

Miyama Tada Baldwincompleted her BSc in social sciences at University College London in 2019. Her interests lie in the crossover between sociology and psychology, particularly how behavior is shaped by social environments. Her final year dissertation explored the relationship between social media use and rising loneliness rates in young people in the UK. Upon completing her studies she embarked upon a research internship in consumer behavior at a research and strategy consultancy in London. She now lives in Italy where she works for a market research company.

Julie Chen is a family physician jointly appointed as Associate Professor (Teaching) in the Department of Family Medicine and Primary Care and the Bau Institute of Medical and Health Sciences Education, who also serves as Assistant Dean (Learner Wellbeing) in the LKS Faculty of Medicine. Her teaching and research focus on the development of medical student professionalism and humanism in undergraduate medical education as well as the exploration of issues affecting doctor and medical student health. In recognition of her work, she has been awarded a Faculty Teaching Medal and two University Outstanding Teaching Awards from the University of Hong Kong.

Amarachi Chukwu is a PhD student in Gender, Feminist & Women's Studies at York University in Toronto. Her main research interests center on Black diaspora and Black feminist intervention in liberation practices. She is also interested in interventions within the academy to transform it into a safe learning environment for marginalized peoples. She holds an MA in Gender Studies and Feminist Research from McMaster University and a BA in Psychology from the University of British Columbia, Vancouver.

Ashley Ferrell was an Elementary Education Major at Berea College, Class of 2019, from Kingsport, Tennessee. She was the Student Supervisor for the Educational Technology Help Desk at Hutchins Library and the Co-Chair of the Teacher Preparation Accountability Committee. She is interested in pedagogy that improves student engagement and retention in addition to focusing on the different learning styles of each student. Ashley currently works as a second grade teacher.

Ashly Fuller completed a BSc Social Sciences at University College London in 2019 and is currently graduating with a Master's in Comparative Social Policy at the University of Oxford. Her main area of interest lies at the intersection of social policy and technology. Her undergraduate dissertation investigated the relationship between trust and accountability in UK charities and innovative technologies such as blockchain and cryptocurrency. Today, her master's thesis evaluates the impact of EU digital inclusion skills policies and explores their effect on cross-national digital inequality. Previously an intern in UK Civil Service, she is looking forward to joining public service before pursuing her studies at a PhD level.

Angela Gennocro was a Biology Major and Management Minor at Florida Gulf Coast University, where she received her B.S. in 2019. She is interested in education and international volunteer work.

Omar Hallab is a third-year BSc Social Sciences student, graduating in 2020. He is passionate about students taking control of their education, and shaping their own experiences. In the true spirit of interdisciplinarity on his degree, he has developed interests in psychology and sociology. With research experience both within and outside of academics, he hopes to pursue further education and research opportunities after his undergraduate studies.

John Ho is a sixth-year medical student in the University of Hong Kong, graduating in 2020. Prior to pursuing his career in the medical field, John was an investment banker in bulge bracket banks specialized in structured finance and derivatives, advising listed corporations across Asia Pacific. John has been actively participating in numerous improvement initiatives of the Faculty on infrastructure, teaching, and learning over the years while serving externally in community medicine initiatives on poverty alleviation. John graduated with honors from the University of Oxford with an undergraduate master's degree in Engineering, Economics and Management in 2010, where he founded and served as president of two international student organizations with primary focuses in finance and education for the underprivileged.

Dionna Jenkins is an English major, Class of 2020, at Smith College. She has held leadership roles, including at Breakthrough Greater Boston (teaching fellow), Urban Education Initiative (academic coach), and Urban Education Fellows Program (teaching fellow). She is committed to effecting profound change in the field of education, particularly by remedying issues of access, equity, and achievement for underserved students, educators, and the institutions and systems charged with supporting them.

Kim Jones is an Associate Professor of Chemical Engineering at McMaster University, where she does research in the body's response to implanted biomaterials—and in issues of inclusion in engineering. She has served as the Engineering Leadership Fellow (focusing on inclusion), the Chair of the Women in Engineering Committee, Associate Chair (Undergraduate) of Chemical Engineering and is an Engineers Canada 30x30 Champion. She is the Chair of the Ontario Network of Women in Engineering (ONWiE), which drives and coordinates province-wide efforts to recruit a diverse population into the study of engineering. She has been a feminist since birth and enthusiastically drives outreach, equity, and inclusion efforts.

Ayushi Kar is third-year student in BSc Social Sciences with Quantitative Methods. Her interests primarily lie in the fields of public policy, economics of technology, and behavior from a quantitative lens. She is currently interested in pursuing her dissertation in Indian innovation policy.

Amrita Kaur is a senior lecturer at the School of Education and Modern Language at Universiti Utara Malaysia (UUM). She teaches postgraduate courses in Educational Psychology and Educational Research Methodology. Her research interests include teaching, learning, and assessment in higher education, students as partners, learning motivation and engagement with a special focus on the self-determination theory. She serves as an editorial member of *Malaysian Journal of Learning and Instruction* and *International Journal of Students as Partners*.

Ali Leota is a bachelor of health student majoring in population health, policy and service delivery at Victoria University of Wellington in New

Zealand. He is the founder and current National President of Tauira Pasifika, the national students' association for Pacific Island students in New Zealand's tertiary education sector. Through his community involvement he has developed a passion to ensure student voices are a valued part of the decision-making process across higher education, and when he graduates in 2020 he wants to pursue further education to contribute to building greater capacity of indigenous academics.

Iska Naaman is a recent graduate of Kaye Academic College of Education in Beer Sheva, Israel, where she trained to become an elementary school teacher, specializing in Bible Studies and Literature, and participated in the college's first pedagogical partnership project. Iska now works as a full-time teacher in a school in the city.

Doron Narkiss is a lecturer in the English Department at Kaye Academic College of Education, teaching English literature to students studying to be English teachers. His research interests include postcolonial literature, TESOL, EIL, and intercultural online learning. He participated in the college's first pedagogical partnership project.

Amanda Eugair Peach is an Instruction Librarian and Assistant Director of Library Services at Berea College's Hutchins Library. She has a Master of Library Science degree from the University of Kentucky and a Master of Higher Education Administration from the University of Louisville. Her research interests are student labor, zines, graphic novels, and the research habits of undergraduates. She is the mother of three amazing girls who keep her laughing.

Katie Quy is a lecturer in psychology and Admissions Tutor for BSc Social Sciences, in the Department of Social Sciences at University College London. She earned her PhD from University of London, and her research interests include social and emotional wellbeing in childhood and adolescence, with a particular focus on coping.

John Straussberger is an Assistant Professor of History at Florida Gulf Coast University. His research focuses on African socialism and nationalism in post-colonial West Africa, as well as the digital humanities.

Kathryn Sutherland is an academic (faculty) developer in the Centre for Academic Development at Victoria University of Wellington in New Zealand. She is an award-winning teacher and researcher whose research and practice has three main areas of focus: the experiences of early career academics, holistic academic development, and working in partnership with students to improve teaching and learning.

Tina Wildhagen, Associate Professor of Sociology at Smith College, earned her doctorate from the University of Iowa, and has won several teaching awards and fellowships. Her research focuses on inequities in students' higher education experiences, with a particular focus on first-generation students. She has been teaching at Smith for over ten years and has worked actively during that time to cultivate classroom cultures where students actively participate in the work of the class.

Toh Yong Bing is a full-time master's student at the School of Education and Modern Language at Universiti Utara Malaysia (UUM). He has many years of experience working with emerging adults from three different Southeast Asia countries outside academia and is passionate about adult learning in higher education. His dissertation which is underway, aims to investigate the role of socio-psychological factors in shaping the development of emerging adults. He is also interested in participating in and exploring the issues related to students as partners.

Yasira Waqar is an assistant professor in the School of Education at Lahore University of Management Sciences (LUMS) Pakistan. She is also faculty lead for professional development at LUMS Learning Institute. During her career, she has taught university-level courses in education technology and research and has worked as a consultant on several national and international projects. Her research focuses on meaningful use of technology to augment student learning, and in applying cognitive psychology to inculcate thinking skills in students. She is also a former US Certified school teacher, with several years of teaching experience in Pakistan and the United States. Yasira is also a trained speech-language pathologist and has worked closely with children with special needs in Pakistan and UAE.

Lightning Source UK Ltd.
Milton Keynes UK
UKHW010452250820
368775UK00006B/245